22 PROVOCATIVE CANADIANS
In the Spirit of Bob Edwards

FOREWORD BY CATHERINE FORD

EDITED BY KERRY LONGPRÉ AND MARGARET DICKSON

Bayeux Arts

Text Copyright © 1999 by Kerry Longpré and Margaret Dickson

Published by:

Bayeux Arts, Inc.
Calgary, Alberta, Canada

Cover photograph: NA-450-1 courtesy of Glenbow Archives
Cover design by Boldface Technologies Inc.
Design by Rachel Hershfield/RH Design
Typeset in Centaur and Frutiger

Canadian Cataloguing in Publication Data

ISBN: 1-896209-45-9
1. Short essays, Canadian (English)*
2. Canadian non fiction (English) – 20th century* I. Longpré, Kerry. II. Dickson, Margaret.
III. Title: Twenty-two provocative Canadians
PS8321.T96 1999 C813'.0108054 C99-911098-5
PR9197.32.T92 1999

First Printing: November 1999

Printed in Canada

The Publisher gratefully acknowledges the financial support of the Canada Council for the Arts, the Alberta Foundation for the Arts, and the Government of Canada through the Book Publishing Industry Development Program.

ACKNOWLEDGEMENTS

In the course of our involvement on the Board of Directors of Alberta Theatre Projects, one of our favourite events has been the annual Bob Edwards Luncheon and Award. We and the theatre company are proud to have honoured many remarkable Canadians with the Bob Edwards Award. The 25th Anniversary of the luncheon seemed a propitious time to collect writings from each of the past recipients.

We would like to extend our gratitude to many people who have been involved in the genesis, development and publication of this anthology. The strong, early support from both publisher Ashis Gupta of Bayeux Arts and The Calgary Foundation was most appreciated. The design skills of Jacquie Morris and Delta Embree of Boldface Technologies did justice to Bob Edwards' character and Catherine Ford touched us with a considered, personal Foreword.

The essential foundation of this book was the generous contribution of writings by the 22 past recipients, their families, able assistants and cooperative publishers. Past media support provided by Ken McGoogan of the *Calgary Herald* and Jeff Collins of CBC Radio for the Bob Edwards Luncheon was graciously extended to this anthology. We also thank Rachel Hershfield of RH Design, Colin Bate of Colin Bate Books, Clare Frock and Myrla Bulman for their creative contributions.

The enthusiasm and effort of the Bob Edwards Committee was vital to the success of this book. Our sincere thanks to Judy Boyes, Tara Brister, Terryann Broadhurst, Anne Brown, Linda Hayes, Patti-Anne Kay, Mary Lamond, Mary MacKimmie, Trish Matheson, Sonny Milne and Marilyn Potts. Thank you as well to the staff of Alberta Theatre Projects, especially Pauline Hughes, Judy Lawrence and Bernadette McKelvey.

The selections in this book represent a fascinating group of Canadians. We hope you also enjoy their unique and stimulating coming together to honour the spirit of Bob Edwards.

Kerry Longpré & Margaret Dickson
Calgary, Alberta
September 1999

CONTENTS

FOREWORD   1

I. ON THE BURDENS OF BEING A WRITER

Pierre Berton   5
Margaret Atwood   10
John Ralston Saul   19
Carol Shields   26
W.O. Mitchell   32

II. ON INTRIGUING CHARACTERS

Grant MacEwan   39
Mordecai Richler   46
Peter C. Newman   51
June Callwood   54
Peter Gzowski   58
James MacGregor   66

III. ON THE IMPORTANCE OF HONEST JOURNALISM

Hugh Dempsey   75
David Suzuki   81
James Gray   89
Lise Bissonnette   93
Andy Russell   99
Patrick Watson   103

IV. ON PASSIONATE DEVOTION TO AN IDEA

Knowlton Nash   115
Jack Webster   121
Jack Peach   127
René Lévesque   132
Allan Fotheringham   140

PERMISSIONS   144

FOREWORD

These words don't come easily, because each is wrung from a place somewhere in my heart that is filled with envy, awe and admiration. Each word must also go through the sieve of jealousy, the dark side of envy that wishes I could have written some of the millions of words Canadian writers have produced that have a life of their own and will live after them, as long as there is voracious appetite to read the printed word.

Conventional wisdom does not grant much of a half-life to newspaper columns. They are products of their time and circumstance. Nonetheless, some of the writers in this book are columnists and journalists; some are novelists; others are essayists. A few are all things to all media.

But all have one thing in common—a fierce desire to connect, through the written word, with a community. As Milan Kundera says about writing in *The Book of Laughter and Forgetting*: "... everyone has trouble accepting the fact he will disappear unheard of and unnoticed in an indifferent universe and everyone wants to make himself into a universe of words before it's too late."

It is that universe of words that connects us all.

We are all linked, some more closely than others.

All of my career, I have been emboldened by the forceful opinions of the mentor of this book—Bob Edwards—whose legendary blunt writing makes today's newspapers pale in comparison. Edwards was outrageous. I wanted to be. I believed, as a young reporter at the *Calgary Herald*, that one day, I could be outrageous. I, too, would be forthright in my opinions; would have a newspaper column. Much of what I wanted has come to pass.

You see, I believed there was a psychic—albeit exceedingly thin—link between the turn-of-the-century newspaperman and the turn-of-this-century newspaperwoman.

Edwards' name was not only folklore in the newspaper community, but in our house.

When Edwards died in 1922, he held a Calgary seat as an MLA in the Alberta legislature. His vacant seat was contested by Clinton J. Ford, my grandfather, who was roundly defeated by the editor of *The Albertan*, the man grandfather called "my friend, W. L. Davidson."

Perhaps there is irony, or at least some harmonics in such circumstances that link us all together. Maybe only a writer—or newspaper columnist—would see such links.

But even as it seems that newspaper and column writing is a creature of the moment in time, a poor cousin to biography, a limp sister to analysis, I've discovered what I thought was outrage is the outer manifestation of care. The tough broad I thought I was has become—indeed, always was, say friends—the marshmallow who cared too much about too much.

That caring about community, that need to record the moment is essentially what all writers do regardless of form. We may hector and rail; question and pontificate; cajole and soothe—each in a distinct voice that is characteristic of an individual personality. But each of us is responsible for part of the collective memory.

The writers in this anthology are all famous Canadians. But I am reminded of Edwards' sardonic view, in 1920, of what would eventually be known as Can-Lit: "Fame, from a literary point of view, consists in having people know you have written a lot of stuff they haven't read."

Luckily, all of the writers who follow have written a lot of stuff everyone has read.

Catherine Ford
Calgary, Alberta
September 1999

I. ON THE BURDENS OF BEING A WRITER

PIERRE BERTON

Journalist, broadcaster, and prolific writer on major events
and icons in Canadian history, PIERRE BERTON exemplifies
the art of informing without becoming pedantic. Berton
admires Bob Edwards for exhibiting the same trait. Often
using humour to engage them, Edwards never relented in his
zeal to ensure his readers knew the truth of a matter.

No other Westerner managed to capture the buoyant, restless, iconoclastic spirit of the West in the way that Bob Edwards did. The country has never known—probably will never know—a publication as outrageous, as irreverent, or as ebullient as his personal creation, the Calgary *Eye-Opener*. Among the so-called legitimate dailies, the *Calgary Herald* had no rival for flamboyance. But there were times when the weekly *Eye-Opener* made the *Herald* seem like a Sunday School tract.

The essence of the paper's appeal was that in an era when journalists could be bribed for a pittance, when newspapers shamelessly distorted the truth, when publishers were caught in political scandals, when editors kowtowed to politicians, stuffed shirts, property interests, and advertisers, Robert Chambers Edwards was ruthlessly honest, ruggedly independent, and totally fearless. More than that, he was very funny.

He pricked balloons, jeered at the newly rich, attacked the bluestockings, poked fun at boosterism, jibed at humbug and bombast. His paper struck a chord with those settlers who had fled the bureaucracy of Europe, the snobbery of England, or the hypocrisy of the Eastern Canadian establishment. It tickled them when Edwards attacked Harry Corby's elevation to the Senate because he made bad whiskey or wrote that "the CPR, Clifford Sifton and the Almighty comprise the Trinity of Canada, ranking in importance in the order named."

In an era when a circulation of seventy-five hundred was considered hugely profitable, the *Eye-Opener* reached a peak of thirty-five thousand. It could make and unmake politicians. R.B. Bennett ascribed his federal defeat in 1904 to Edwards. The mayor of Calgary refused to run for re-election when the *Eye-Opener* opposed him. No wonder Edwards made enemies. At one point the *Eye-Opener* was denied the mails. The CPR banned it from its trains. The ministerial association attacked it. Edwards was even challenged to a duel. But he prevailed, even though his paper often missed several issues in a row and rejected advertising for any product Edwards felt he couldn't support. He was more than a humorist; he was a genuine prairie reformer, "a Robin Hood of the pen" in the words of the Winnipeg jurist Roy St. George Stubbs. He opposed restrictive divorce laws and Sunday blue laws, was sympathetic to prostitutes, suffragists, and trade unions, and regularly exposed shady and fraudulent deals, some of them the work of community pillars.

His greatest appeal was his refusal to take himself or his newspaper seriously, although he was deadly serious in his attacks on grafting politicians and rapacious real estate interests. He once wrote that the three biggest liars in Alberta were "Robert Chambers–Gentleman; Honourable A.L. Sifton–Premier; and Bob Edwards–Editor." Arthur Sifton tried to sue him for that, whereupon Edwards offered to collaborate in a joint suit since Edwards, the Editor, had also slandered Chambers, the Gentleman. The Premier quickly retreated. Another public figure who threatened suit but thought better of it was the austere High Commissioner to Great Britain, Lord Strathcona.

Those who knew Bob Edwards from the *Eye-Opener* alone might be pardoned for conjuring up an image of him as a wild-eyed roisterer, slapping backs in local saloons, as fiery and as loud as his paper, always at the centre of the crowd. He was anything but that—the direct antithesis, in fact, of the image he projected in print. He was a plump, bright-eyed, rumpled man with a sparse, sandy moustache, who dressed in sombre suits and sported a wing collar. He was diffident, uneasy in a crowd, and taciturn with any but a small circle of friends. Nobody could persuade him to make a public speech. Like an actor who exists through his stage roles, he came to life only in the columns of his paper.

He had more culture in his big toe than most of Calgary's upstart establishment exhibited in their entire bodies. He was a lover of the theatre, of music, and, above all, of good literature. Before he was thirty he had seen most of Europe and had even edited a small journal on the Riviera. He had experienced the watering places of the gentry and wanted no part of them; instead, he chose Calgary and the long bar of the Alberta Hotel.

He himself hit up the booze, hard and often, and made no secret of it. "Every man has his favorite bird," he wrote. "Mine is the bat." He was not a steady drinker, but when he fell off the wagon—"leaped" would be a better word—he landed hard. During those sprees the *Eye-Opener* failed to publish and the whole town knew that Edwards was drunk. There were others in Calgary who drank as much, but they did not proclaim it to the world.

It is said of Edwards that if he had not taken to drink he might have been a Canadian Mark Twain or, had he stayed in Europe, he would almost certainly have become a major literary figure. Perhaps in those rare moments of self-examination that led to the inevitable spree and the inevitable drying out at Holy Cross Hospital, Edwards himself contemplated those possibilities. If he did, he missed the point. Although his work has escaped the dubious immortality of the school text, he was the Canadian Mark Twain; he became and remains a major literary figure. He is constantly being rediscovered, anthologized, eulogized. His aphorisms have stood the test of time.

On October 6, 1908, three weeks before the federal election, Daniel McGillicuddy's *Calgary News* launched a personal attack on Edwards that for virulence and savagery has never been equalled in Canada. The attack took the form of a two-column letter on the front page, written by McGillicuddy but signed "Nemesis." It referred to the *Eye-Opener* as "a disreputable sheet, the mission of which has been blackmail and the contents of which [are] ... slander and smut." It called Edwards a "ruffian," a "moral leper," and a "skunk ... whose literary fulminations cannot but create the impression that he was born in a brothel and bred on a dungpile." That was only the beginning. Edwards was "a four flusher," "a tin horn," and "a welcher on poker debts." Nemesis promised more in future issues: "I intend to show that he is a libeller, a character thief, a coward, a liar, a drunkard, a dope-fiend, and a degenerate." Nemesis promised to prove all these charges, but before the next issue appeared a shaken Edwards had, with the help of his friend, the lawyer Paddy Nolan, sued McGillicuddy for libel.

The trial made national headlines. McGillicuddy could not prove his charges, and after five hours of deliberation, the jury found for Edwards. Alas, it was a pyrrhic victory. McGillicuddy was fined a nominal one hundred dollars without having to pay costs. The jury expressed disapproval of the *Eye-Opener's* stories, and the judge rebuked Edwards, describing the paper's articles with such words as "debasing and demoralizing." None of this had any effect on the *Eye-Opener's* fortunes. The paper's circulation increased while the *News* foundered; a few months later McGillicuddy sold the paper and vanished from the scene.

In 1917, at the age of fifty-three, Bob Edwards the lifelong bachelor married Kate Penman, a twenty-four-year-old girl from Glasgow. It was not a successful marriage; Edwards was too set in his ways, nor would he modify his drinking. But drunk or sober he had become a Calgary fixture, a member of the establishment, a vibrant symbol of the West's adolescent years, and, by 1921, a successful provincial politician. McGillicuddy was dead, but Edwards was unforgiving. "Is it not remarkable," he wrote to a friend, "that here I am in the Legislature and McGillicuddy is in Hell." Shortly after that, on November 14, 1922, he died of influenza at the age of fifty-eight. His paper, which more than any other had captured the Western spirit, died with him.

MARGARET ATWOOD

MARGARET ATWOOD is a tireless advocate for writers, a
vocation evidenced by her long involvement with PEN
International, among many related commitments.
Championing the essential right of a writer to freedom of
speech, and the public's essential need to read them, she
defies the stereotype of the quiet writer working in isolation.

Margaret Atwood

In 1972, I wrote and published a book called *Survival: A Thematic Guide to Canadian Literature*, which ignited a ferocious debate and became, as they say, a runaway bestseller. This was a shock to everyone, including me. Canadian writing, interesting? Among the bulk of readers at that time it was largely unknown and among the cognoscenti it was frequently treated as a dreary joke, an oxymoron, a big yawn, or the hole in a non-existent doughnut.

At the beginning of the '60s, the usual sales of poetry books numbered in the hundreds, and a novel was doing well if it hit a thousand copies. But over that decade, things changed rapidly. After the wartime '40s and the beige '50s, Canada was showing a renewed interest in its own cultural doings. The Canada Council began supporting writers in earnest in 1965. In Quebec, the Quiet Revolution had generated an outburst of literary activity; in the ROC (the Rest Of Canada as we call it now but did not then) many poets had emerged through coffee houses and public readings, more novelists and short-story writers were becoming known, and Expo 67, the Montreal world's fair, had created a fresh national self-confidence.

Audiences had been building steadily, and by 1972 there was a critical mass of readers who wanted to hear more; and thus, through a combination of good luck, good timing, and good reviews, *Survival* became an "overnight publishing sensation," and I myself became an instant sacred monster. "Now you're a target," Farley Mowat said to me, "and they will shoot at you."

How prescient he was. Who could have suspected that this modest cultural artifact would have got so thoroughly up the noses of my elders and betters? If the book had sold the 3,000 copies initially projected, nobody would have bothered their heads much about it, but in the first year alone it sold ten times that number, and suddenly CanLit was everybody's business. The few dedicated academic souls who had cultivated this neglected pumpkin patch over the meagre years were affronted because a mere chit of a girl had appropriated a pumpkin they regarded as theirs, and the rest were affronted because I had obnoxiously pointed out that there was in fact a pumpkin to appropriate. Even now, after 27 years, some Jack or Jackess emerges with seasonal regularity to take one more crack at *moi*, the supposed Giant, in a never-ending game of Let Us Now Blame Famous Women. You get to feel like the mechanical duck at the fun-fair shooting gallery, though no one has won the oversized panda yet, because I still seem to be quacking.

Over the years, I've been accused of just about everything, from bourgeois superstition to communist rabble-rousing to not being Marshall McLuhan. (I would have liked to have been Marshall McLuhan—it seemed a ton o' fun—but he seemed to have the job pretty much cornered.) Yet when I was writing this book— or rather when I was putting it together, for it was more an act of synthesis than of authorship—I attached no particular importance to it. I was, after all, a poet and novelist, wasn't I? I did not consider myself a real critic—just a kind of bake-sale muffin lady, doing a little cottage-industry fund-raising in a worthy cause.

The worthy cause was The House of Anansi Press, a small literary publisher formed in 1967 by writers Dennis Lee and David Godfrey as a response to the dearth of publishing opportunities for new writing at that time. Anansi was diverse in scope—Austin Clarke, Harold Sonny Ladoo, Roch Carrier and Jacques Ferron were some of its authors—and had already made quite a few waves by 1971, when Dennis, an old college friend, buttonhooked me onto its board. So there we were one grey November day, a tiny, intrepid, overworked, underpaid band, glumly contemplating the balance sheet, which showed an alarming amount of red ink. Publishing Rule No. 1 is that it's hard to keep small literary publishers solvent unless you have the equivalent of knitting books to support them.

To pay the bills, Anansi had begun a line of user-friendly self-help guides, which had done moderately well: *Law Law Law*, by Clayton Ruby and Paul Copeland, which set forth how to disinherit your relatives, avoid being bled dry by your estranged spouse, and so forth; and *VD*, one of the first venereal disease books, which explicated unwanted goo and warts and such, though AIDS was still a decade into the future.

Thus was born *Survival*. As I'd travelled the country's byways, giving poetry readings and toting cardboard boxes of my own books to sell afterwards because often enough there was no bookstore, the absence of views on the subject was spectacular. The two questions I was asked most frequently by audience members were "Is there any Canadian literature?" and, "Supposing there is, isn't it just a second-rate copy of real literature, which comes from England and the United States?" In Australia they called this attitude the Cultural Cringe; in Canada it was the Colonial Mentality. In both—and in many smaller countries around the world, as it turned out—it was part of a tendency to believe that the Great Good Place was, culturally speaking, elsewhere.

Through no fault of my own, I happened to be doing a one-year teaching stint at York University. Canadian Literature formed part of the course load, so I'd had to come up with some easily grasped approaches to it—easily grasped by me as well as by my students, because I was, by training, a Victorianist, and had never formally studied Canadian literature. (Not surprising: it wasn't taught.) I discovered that previous thinkers on the subject, although pithy enough, had been few in number: there was not exactly a wealth of existing lore.

Back to the Anansi meeting. "Hey, I know," I cried, in my Mickey Rooneyish way. "Let's do a *VD* of Canadian literature!" What I meant, I explained, was a sort of handbook for the average reader—for all those people I'd met on my tours who'd wanted to know more, but didn't know where to start. This book would not be for academics. It would have no footnotes, and would not employ the phrase "on the other hand," or at least not much. It would also contain lists of other books that people could actually go into a bookstore and buy. This was a fairly revolutionary concept, because the CanLit of the past was mostly out of print, and that of the present was kept well hidden at the back of the store, in among the Beautiful Canadiana fall foliage calendars.

We now take it for granted that Canadian literature exists as a category, but this proposition was not always self-evident. To have any excuse for being, the kind of book I had in mind would have to prove several points. First, that, yes, there was a Canadian literature—such a thing did indeed exist. (This turned out to be a radical proposition at the time, and was disputed by many when the book appeared.) Second, that this body of work was not just a second-rate version of English or American, or, in the case of Francophone books, of French literature, but that it had different preoccupations which were specific to its own history and geopolitics. This too was a radical proposition, although common sense ought to have indicated that it was just common sense: if you were a rocky, watery northern country, cool in climate, large in geographical expanse, small but diverse in population, and with a huge aggressive neighbour to the south, why wouldn't you have concerns that varied from those of the huge aggressive neighbour? Or indeed from those of the crowded, history-packed, tight little island, recently but no longer an imperial power, that had once ruled the waves? Well, you'd think they'd be different, wouldn't you? To justify the teaching of Canadian literature as such, you'd still have to start from the same axioms: i) it exists, and ii) it's distinct.

Back to the Anansi meeting. The desperate will try anything, so the board agreed that this idea should be given a whirl. Over the next four or five months, I wrote away at it, and as I finished each section Dennis Lee edited it, and under Dennis's blue pencil the book grew from the proposed hundred-page handbook to a length of 246 pages. It also took on a more coherent shape and direction. The book's subtitle—*A Thematic Guide to Canadian Literature*—meant that we were aiming, not at an all-inclusive cross-indexed survey such as was provided in 1997 by the 1,199-page *Oxford Companion to Canadian Literature*, nor at a series of studies of this author or that, nor at a collection of New-critical close readings or *explications du texte*. We were doing the sort of thing that art historian Nikolaus Pevsner had done in *The Englishness of English Art*, or that the American literary critics Perry Miller and Leslie Fiedler were doing in their examinations of American literature: the identification of a series of characteristics and leitmotifs, and a comparison of the varying treatments of them in different national and cultural environments.

For example: money as a sign of divine grace or providence is present in the American tradition from the Puritans through Benjamin Franklin through *Moby-Dick* through Henry James through *The Great Gatsby*. The theme is treated now seriously, now cynically, now tragically, now ironically, just as a leitmotif in a symphony may be played in different keys and in different tempos. It varies as time unrolls and circumstances change, of course: the 18th century is not the 20th. Yet the leitmotif persists as a dominating concern—a persistent cultural obsession, if you like.

The persistent cultural obsession of Canadian literature, said *Survival*, was, well, survival. In actual life, and in both the Anglophone and the Francophone sectors, this concern is often enough a factor of the weather, as when the ice storm cuts off the electrical power. *La survivance* has long been an overt theme in Quebec political life, currently manifesting itself as anxiety about the survival of French. In the ROC, it's more like a nervous tic: what'cher gonner do when free trade trashes your ability to control your water supply, or when the Mounties sell themselves to Disneyland, or when your government says that the magazines from the huge, aggressive neighbour to the south are the same as yours really, or when there's a chance that after the next Quebec referendum, that part of the country will no longer be that part of the country? And so on and so forth.

Survival, therefore, began with this dominant note. It then postulated a number of other motifs in Canadian literature—motifs that either did not exist at all in one of the literatures chosen for comparison (for instance, there are almost no "Indians" in English novels), or which did exist, but were not handled in the same way. The Canadian "immigrant story," from fleeing Loyalists, to Scots kicked off their land, to starving Irish, to Latvians emigrating after the Second World War, to the economic refugees of the '70s and '80s, tends to be very different from the one told by Americans: none of their stories is likely to say that the immigrants were really trying to get into Canada but ended up in the United States *faute de mieux*. Canada has rarely been the promised land. About the closest we've come is the title of Wayne Johnson's 1998 novel, *The Colony of Unrequited Dreams*.

The tradition identified in *Survival* was not a bundle of uplifting Pollyanna cheer: quite the reverse. CanLit, at least up until 1970, was on balance a somewhat dour concoction. Some critics who couldn't read very well—a widespread occupational hazard, it seems—thought I was somehow *advocating* this state of affairs. *Au contraire*: if the book has attitude, it's more like you are here, you really do exist and this is where, so pull up your socks and quit whining. As Alice Munro says, "Do what you want and live with the consequences." Or as *Survival* itself says in its last chapter, "Having bleak ground under your feet is better than having no ground at all … a tradition doesn't necessarily exist to bury you: it can also be used as material for new departures."

Many things have happened in the 27 years since *Survival* was published. In politics, the Quebec cliffhanger and loss of national control and increased U.S. domination brought about by free trade have become, not the tentative warning notes they were in *Survival*, but everyday realities. Canada's well-known failure to embrace a single "identity" of the yodelling or Beefeater variety has come to seem less like a failure than a deliberate and rather brave refusal. In literary criticism, Regionalism, Feminism, Deconstructionism, Political Correctness, Appropriation of Voice, and Identity Politics have all swept across the scene, leaving their traces. The former Canadian-identity question, "Where is here?" has been replaced by "Who are we?" "Discourse" and "text" are the new words for "debate" and "book." "Problematize" has became a verb, "postmodern"—once a cutting-edge adjective— is used to describe kicky little handbags, and obfuscation, in some academic quarters, has become a mode of being.

Survival, the book, seemed quainter and more out-of-date as these various years went by, and—incidentally—as its wishes were granted and its predictions realized. Yet its central concerns remain with us, and must still be confronted. Are we really that different from anybody else? If so, how? And is that how something worth pre-serving? In 1972, *Survival* concluded with two questions: *Have we survived? If so, what happens after Survival?* We're still asking the same questions.

People often ask me what I would change about *Survival* if I were writing it today. The obvious answer is that I wouldn't write it today, because I wouldn't need to. The thing I set out to prove has been proven beyond a doubt: few would seri-ously argue, any more, that there is no Canadian literature. The other answer is that I wouldn't be able to write it, not only because of my own hardening brain, but because the quantity, range and diversity of books now published would defeat any such effort. Mordecai Richler's well-known jest, "world-famous in Canada," ceased to be such a laugh—many Canadian writers are now world-famous, period. The erstwhile molehill of CanLit has grown to a mountain. The year-old, fully bilingual Institute for Canadian Studies at the University of Ottawa lists some 279 Canadian studies centres located in other countries, including 20 in France, 65 in the United States, 16 in Germany and 22 in India. Canadian writers regularly achieve foreign publication, win major prizes, sign movie deals. In fact, so voguish is Canadian writing—or writing in English, at least—that it's become almost embarrassing.

All the more curious that Lucien Bouchard, visiting Paris in March, would quip that he had never seen Canadian culture walking along the street, "but apparently it exists in Ottawa." Of course you don't see much walking along the street if what you're looking at is not the bookstore window, but your own reflection in it. Though even M. Bouchard's reflection is "Canadian culture," considering his status as that archetypical folkloric bogey, the vengeful Scissors Man, used from time immemorial to frighten the fractious: *If you don't sit down and shut up, M. Bouchard will climb in through your window at night and SEPARATE you!*

In Canadian culture, however, there's always a negative side. At present we have cuts to grants, threats to magazines, publishers in peril through withdrawal of funding, writers struggling with the effects upon their royalties of book-chain deep discounting, and so forth—not to mention the homogenizing effect of the global economy. *Have we survived?*

But this is Canada, land of contrasts. Indeed it is Canada, land of rugs: no sooner has a rug been placed beneath the nation's artistic feet than it is pulled out, but no sooner has it been pulled out in one place than it is inserted in another. Now, in an astonishing but gratifying development, Quebec has announced that the first $15,000 of income from copyrights—from songs to books to computer software—will now be tax exempt. (By no great coincidence, $15,000 is the average income from writing in this country.) Will there be unforeseen consequences? Will Quebec become the Ireland of Canada, haven for writers, and the Prague of Europe, the latest chic destination? Will every young, mean and lean creator from all over the country stampede to Montreal, where the rent is cheap and the edible food ditto, so that they can actually have a hope of earning a living from their work? Why stay in

Toronto, where the prices are high, the smog is toxic, your vote is worth only a tenth of a vote in North Bay, the public health system is going to rat excrement, and you get sneered at by your own provincial government and the National Post for being not-rich? Indeed, why stay in Ontario, where culture and the arts are funded at the rate of $39 a head, as opposed to $79 a head in Quebec?

Experience has shown that where bohemia goes, real estate development is sure to follow. First the artists, then the cafés, then the designers, then the lawyers. M. Bouchard must know this: he's been called many things, but rarely stupid. Could it be that this crafty tax move will revitalize downtown Montreal, which for some years has been bleeding at every pore? And revitalize it by means of—*choc, horreur!*—Anglophone Canadian writers—incongruous tax exiles from the ROC?

All M. Bouchard has to do is extend the same kind of tax largesse to the publishing industry, and Montreal may once again become the vital centre of Anglophone Canadian literary activity, as it was in the '40s and '50s. The street along which Bouchard can see Canadian culture walking may soon be his own. In that case, the 21st century answer to the second-last question posed in *Survival* may be—at least as regards writers—both bizarre and deeply ironic:

Have we survived?

Yes. But only in Quebec.

JOHN RALSTON SAUL

One of Canada's most provocative thinkers and visionaries, JOHN RALSTON SAUL challenges academics, the managerial elite, experts on anything, and those who slavishly follow an ideology or process. He acknowledges the power of words and challenges those in control of the written word to act responsibly, while urging everyone to think carefully about what is presented.

It is hardly surprising that those who hold power should attempt to control the words and language people use. Determining how individuals communicate is the best chance rulers have to control what they think. Clumsy men try to do this through violence and fear. Heavy-handed men running heavy-handed systems attempt the same thing through police-enforced censorship. The more sophisticated the elites, the more they concentrate on creating integrated intellectual systems which control expression through the communications structures. These systems require only the discreet use of censorship and uniformed men. In other words, those who take power will always try to change the established language. And those who hold power will try to control it. Governments produced by the most banal of electoral victories, like those produced by the crudest of coups d'état, will always feel obliged to dress themselves up linguistically in some way.

At stake are not simply particular temporary arguments but the entire baggage of a civilization. What a language says about a society's history will create mythology, direct the individual's imagination and limit or justify whatever those in power wish to do. We can recount our own history in a myriad of ways, twisting the origins and characteristics of the individual, the passage of kings, the sequence of wars, the evolution of architecture, the relationship between rich and poor, between men and women to suit whatever is currently at stake. But anyone attempting a disinterested look will notice that each major change in structure is either preceded or rapidly followed by some revolution in language. For the last half century, we have been lost in a jungle of social sciences which claim to have released man from the intellectual manipulations of the past, thanks to the application of disinterested rational analysis. And yet a calm look at any specific subject they have touched reveals that their objectivity has been just another interested manipulation of language.

The wordsmith—prophet, singer, poet, essayist, novelist—has always been either the catalyst of change or, inversely, the servant of established power. He breaks up the old formulas of wisdom or truth and thus frees the human imagination so that individuals can begin thinking of themselves and their society in new ways, which the writer must then express in new language. He may also put himself at the service of the new powers in order to build linguistic cages in which that freed imagination may be locked.

The breakup of the old Western linguistic order began in the fourteenth century, when men like Dante, Petrarch and Chaucer created remarkable social reflections by infusing their local languages with the genius of great poetry. They intentionally set these vulgar tongues in opposition to the Latin of the official religious and intellectual order. This breakup turned into what might be better described as a breakout in the sixteenth and seventeenth centuries, with first the dramatization of reality led by Shakespeare and Molière, then the insidious informality of the essay, which with Michel de Montaigne and Abraham Cowley began questioning the theoretical truths of their time, and finally the birth of a rough and undignified means of communication—the novel. In the hands of a one-armed old soldier like Cervantes and a trouble-making doctor like Rabelais, these simple prose stories created entire models of civilization for every man's imagination—models which reflected reality and not the official portrait of the world order. Finally, in the eighteenth and nineteenth centuries, this novel form came to full strength, poking its reflecting eye into the smallest corners of the established order. From Swift and Voltaire to Goethe, Dickens, Tolstoy and Zola, it mocked and dissected everything from the grand mythologies to the methods of industrial production and the ambitions of a small-town doctor's wife.

The novel was not a product or a creature of reason. It was the most irrational means of communication, subject to no stylistic order or ideological form. It was to intellectual order what animism is to religion—devoid of organized precedence or dependence on social structure. For the purposes of the novelist, everything was alive and therefore worthy of interest and doubt. At its best the novel became a vehicle for humanistic honesty. However, like democracy, it rose in tandem with the forces of reason. The endless specifics of reform made them allies to such a degree that the novel became the dominant linguistic form of the rational revolution.

In that process novelists became famous people and important factors in the process of social evolution. They wrote about every aspect of civilization and, if they had examined a problem seriously and then written well about it in their fiction, they could make an impact on the condition of the peasantry, public education, the morality of empire building or indeed on what women thought about men and men about women.

Most citizens still see our contemporary wordsmiths as an independent voice given more to criticizing the established powers than to praising them. And yet it is hard to think of another era when such a large percentage of the wordsmiths have been so cut off from general society and when language has been so powerless to communicate to the citizens the essence of what is happening around us and to us. The workings of power have never been so shielded by professional verbal obscurantism. The mechanisms of waste disposal management, opera houses, universities, hospitals, of everything to do with science, medicine, agriculture, museums and a thousand other sectors are protected by the breakdown of clear, universal language.

Strangely, writers seem unwilling or unable to attack effectively this professional obscurantism. In fact, the majority actively participate in it. They claim independence from established authority, but accept and even encourage the elitist structures that literature has developed over the last half century. As indignant individuals they rightly criticize power, but as writers they tend to encourage, through their own use of specialized literary forms, the Byzantine layering of language which divides and confuses our society. They have saved from the writer's inheritance his desire to speak out in the name of justice, but many have forgotten that this involves doing so first via their writing. In their rush to become part of rational society, which means to become respected professionals in their own right, they have forgotten that the single most important task of the wordsmith is to maintain the common language as a weapon whose clarity will protect society against the obscurities of power. The professional, by definition, is in society. He has his assigned territory over which his expertise gives him control. The writer is meant to be the faithful witness of everyman and should therefore be neither within society nor without. He must be of society—the constant link between all men.

Novelists had the power to make the new middle-class citizenry dream of freedom. They created a force which could pierce the shield of authority. That force consisted of ideas, situations and emotions clearly communicated. They used this to collapse the credibility of Church dogma and to lay out a path which the nascent democratic regimes could follow. They defined and posted and defended on a continuous basis the standards expected from a responsible citizen. They became the voice of the citizen against the ubiquitous *raison d'état*, which reappeared endlessly to justify everything from unjust laws and the use of child labour to incompetent generalship and inhuman conditions on warships. In places such as Russia, the novelist's was a loud voice widely and constantly heard, leading the way from the

Napoleonic Wars to the Revolution of 1917. Throughout the West these storytellers, along with the poets and the essayists, baited and attacked and mocked again and again those with power and the systems they ran. The themes they popularized have gradually turned into the laws which, for all their flaws, have improved the state of man.

Emotion—so out of favour today in the management of public affairs—was one of the strengths novels used to neutralize the most convincing explanations of state interest and of financial necessity. A great novelist could keep his head up and his words flowing even in the passionate gales produced by the supermen Heroes, who increasingly seized power and wreaked general havoc. Elsewhere in society brilliant and decent men of reason were silenced by these Heroes. Reason, they discovered, eliminated the emotional force necessary to fight back. The novelist could be saved from this trap by his need to communicate with everyman, but also by the need to animate characters who were as real as real men and women. The novelist preached reason but was himself dependent upon common sense, constantly balancing intellect with emotion. He served our imagination through his devotion to clarity and universality. Those wordsmiths who in some way served established power almost always preached complexity and the obscurity of superior language.

With success and influence the novelists kept on multiplying until there were more of them than anyone could have imagined. And so, in the last years of the twentieth century, the citizen stares out expectantly into the vast scribbling crowd in search of the new Tolstoy, Zola's successor, Goethe reborn, Conrad or Lorca, and he does indeed find great writers and great novels. But above all he finds changed expectations, as the writing community is increasingly dominated by intractable purveyors of novels too opaque for any public beyond the semiprofessional reader, bevies of approving or disapproving professors of literature, multiplying hordes produced by creative-writing schools, esoteric sects producing high art of the sort which used to belong in the world of the vanity press and scores of hands rushing out detailed confessions of their personal loves and anxieties. Where the dangerous wordsmith and his weapon—the word—once led, a grand army of introspection, style and literary analysis now holds sway.

It is easy to bemoan a society in which the creative word no longer carries great weight in the large and small arguments of the day. But, citizens rightly ask—What does this person know to merit our ears? Even those writers, great and otherwise, who address the real world in their fiction, find that they are tarred by the broad brush of literature's withdrawal into professionalism and specialization. Perhaps this slide away from reality is simply part of an inevitable decline into dotage. After all, over the last seven hundred years the great centre stage of public communications has been held by a series of quite different dramatic forms. Thus the ballad gave way to the poem; and the poem more or less to the play and to the essay; and both of these to the novel. Now the electronic image is in the process of squeezing the novel out of the limelight. None of these forms ever quite disappears. But they do slip off the centre stage, out of the public's view and into the wings. There they hang about like dissatisfied old troupers, still convinced they could do it better than the newcomers. Yet history has little sympathy for the wordsmith as a delicate flower. And neither fatigue nor intellectual gentility are strong arguments for passivity.

The evolution of language can be reduced to a series of breakouts in the direction of that clarity which allows ideas to be delivered and understanding promoted. Those are the moments when writers explode the established arguments and light up the obscurities of power. Nothing is more terrifying to those in authority, whether their power is over a country, a factory or a child. They quickly launch hunts to recapture this wild language and, once successful, force it back into appropriate order. Two factors are constant: in its moments of freedom, language seeks clarity and communication; when imprisoned, the word instead becomes a complex and obscure shield for those who master it.

Over the last two and a half millennia, Western language has managed three escapes from the prison of established and appropriate order. The first occurred in the city-state of Athens, the second through the person of a young man who preached as the Messiah. The third started out audaciously with the genius of Dante and grew in strength despite constant opposition until it reached a maximum of freedom in the novel. That language now seems perilously close to being recaptured by the forces of order.

CAROL SHIELDS

Carol Shields, the much lauded author of novels about 'ordinary'
people, is cognizant of the vulnerability of novelists who bare
themselves by publishing their own words for the world to read.
Is it a fair price to pay for the empowerment that comes to
careful readers in seeing themselves depicted in literature?

Carol Shields

There was a period in my early life when my friends and I, spurred by romantic yearnings, I suppose, spent great widths of time talking about the possibility and need of "truly knowing someone." This phrase chimed with half a dozen others in our vocabulary: the exposing of the soul, the opening of the heart, the completion of one person by another, and so forth. We believed this kind of appropriative and intimate knowledge was possible, and moreover that it was desirable.

Somewhere along the way I lost faith with the enterprise. What interested me instead was the *unknowability* of others, their very *otherness*, in fact. It was apparent to me that members of close, loving families resisted the forces of coercive revelation, and that even partners in long, happy marriages remained, ultimately, strangers, one to the other. Although we were living in the age of communication, the sixties, the seventies, it became clear that people who "spilled their guts" sacrificed a portion of their dignity in so doing, and that, in any case, what they spilled was suspect, either self-pitying or self-aggrandizing, or else projecting a single, touched-up version of who they were and how they preferred to be registered at a particular moment—for it was understood that a variant self could be brought forward the next day, or even

...hour.

Hughs Marker

...ould be dismayed to discover the limited nature of
...vas heartened, in the same way I was heartened,
...nat the Methodist God, with whom I'd grown up,
...ripple of sensation that passed through my head.
...ed, and stripped bare. To be solitary, that is to be
...ang on to the forces of originality and innocence.
...one; those two austere existential declaratives were
...lthood. But to be alone in the midst of life brought
...le that required a certain amount of philosophical
...remise, in fact, close to unbearable. Human activity
...ity and immobilization was the oxygen I sought. The
...ed me at every level; it was what illuminated my imag-
...y into my novels. My own life—what a sorry admis-
...s not quite enough. I desperately needed to know how
...moved about from room to room in their ordinary
...dinary or extraordinary things they said to each other
...k struck midnight or nine a.m. or noon—even though
...h things as lying side-by-side with the idleness of gossip or in the was....... g of voyeurism.

Judith Gill, the narrator of my first novel *Small Ceremonies*, announces her need openly, that she requires for her survival the narratives of other lives, and that she is willing to suspend judgment and direction and moral imperative in order to do nothing more than peer into the windows of alternate human arrangements. Her need is so strong, in fact, that she becomes a professional biographer, a vocation that allows her to snoop, sniff, interview, eavesdrop, interpret, and bring to ripe conclusion the motives and the figurative possibilities of her subjects.

When I first began writing novels, friends asked me what it was I wrote about. At first I didn't know what to say, for, in fact, I wasn't sure what my subject was. I soon found out—by reading the reviews of my books, and listening to these same friends.

It seemed I wrote about ordinary people—whoever *they* are—and their ordinary, yet occluded, lives. And I also wrote, more and more, about that subjunctive branch of people (mea culpa) who were curious about the details of *other* ordinary people, so curious, in fact, that they became biographers or novelists, those beings who are allowed societal permission to investigate—through the troughs of archival material, through letters and diaries and blurred photographs, by way of offhand conversations and reminiscences and abrupt literary interpolations and fictional thrusts directed at the lives of the famous and the not-at-all famous.

How do we arrive, then, at the lives of others, their presumed kernel of authenticity? As a child I did poorly at mathematics, but enjoyed what we called "story problems." Mary Brown is sent to the grocer's for two pounds of cheese at a dollar and a half a pound. How much change will she get back from a $20 bill? The answer came easily, or not so easily, but it was the tug of biographical curiosity I chiefly felt. Who was this Mary Brown and what was she doing with all that cheese? Was she old enough to be trusted with a $20 bill? And what of her wider dreams and aspirations, or even her immediate thoughts as she skipped home with her sack of groceries and her pocketful of coins?

I remember trying to "interview" my Canadian mother-in-law when she was in her eighties, wanting to access a portion of the childhood she had spent on a pioneer farm in Manitoba. The project was doomed from the beginning. I didn't know the right questions, and she didn't have any idea what I wanted to know. My line of inquiry, even to my own ears, felt intrusive and inappropriate, and her answers were, not surprisingly, vague and, for my purposes, not at all useful. What I hoped for was the precise inch-by-inch texture of that early 20th century Icelandic farmhouse located on a threadlike river sixty miles north of Winnipeg, the furniture, the floor coverings, the ceiling, the ornaments that rested on the rough kitchen shelves. What I got were generalities: "Well, it was homey. Well, we made our own cheese. The sheep, they were a bother. It was cold in winter." In short, the experiment was a failure. I half expected it would be.

There is something oddly shaming about possessing too avid a sense of curiosity. I remember once seeing a young man seated in his front garden. Before him was an ironing board, and on the ironing board a small manual typewriter. He was tapping away with such excitement that he didn't look up as I passed by. I wanted to stop on the spot and besiege him with questions: What are you writing? Why such concentration of energy? Let me see what you're working on.

Naturally when I find myself on buses or trains I feel a compulsion to know the titles of the books my fellow passengers are reading. And when I am being interviewed about one of my books, I often find myself interviewing back: How did you happen to become a journalist? What sort of articles are you usually assigned? Do you have any children? Tell me more.

More is what the indecently curious always want. They want the *details*, and no detail is too small to be of interest.

But we live in a society that forbids the intimate interrogating of strangers. Inquisitive people are discouraged and certainly disparaged. Journalists and biographers may be given special privileges, allowed to ask their Nosy Parker questions, but the rest of us are forced to deal imaginatively with the great gaps.

For novelists this means observing, eavesdropping, gently probing, but, in the end, risking ourselves and our small truths, guessing at the way other people live and think, hoping to get it right at least part of the time.

And I long ago understood that the silences our society imposes give to the novelist a freshness of opportunity, a way to bring spaciousness and art into the smallest, most "ordinary" lives. Even so, I suffer, as many writers do, from a scavenger's guilt and always experience a desire to include on the title page of my books some small message of acknowledgment: "Forgive me." Or "I'm sorry."

Writers, so willing to interpret the material of the world become remarkably sensitive when the world wants to interpret them. I have never learned, for instance, what to say when journalists ask my age. I don't want to be coy and I don't want to lie, but I have yet to understand the relevance of the inquiry, and I suspect male authors are not interrogated in the same manner. "What an *interesting* and *curious* question," I long to purr. Sometimes I reply in French: numbers have a way of softening in the gel of that beautiful language. My daughter suggests I reply with one of those old fashioned algebra problems: "I'm twice as old as my nephew's mother, divided by the annual salary of my husband, times the number of home runs in the most recent World Series ball game, minus the number of molars I've lost over the years."

I am also sensitive to what I call the post-publication frenzies. There is no more vulnerable time in a writer's life than the month or so following a new book. It is not the critics who offend; it is the friends. Friends mean to be kind, but they lack tact. "When will your book come out in paperback?" they demand slyly. And there are the friends who say, "I've bought your book, but I haven't had a chance to read it yet." *Haven't had a chance! What does this mean?* There is always someone who says, "I've especially requested your book at the library." (This is pronounced as though it were a form of high tribute.) Someone once wounded me by saying, "I read your book between dinner and bedtime last night," not honouring in any way the three years I'd spent writing it. The funniest thing ever said to me came from one of my colleagues. "I would have bought your book, Carol, but it came out too late for my wife's birthday." Like most women writers I hear often that so-and-so's wife reads my books; a vacuum follows this declaration; indeed there is no civil response. Nor is there a response to those who say they too would write novels if only they had the time.

One thinks of J.B. Priestly, who, when he came to write his autobiography, titled it *I Had Time*.

Something strange happened to me when my first book was published. I was suddenly invited to give "talks," I who had no experience or talent for "talks." I was asked to address book clubs or meetings of salespersons or Seniors' groups. What on earth might I talk about? I asked one of my writer friends for ideas. "Why don't I lend you *my* talk," she said. Wonderful! I asked her what her talk was called. "The Writer as Masochist," she replied.

And, yet, for all the trials of being a writer, I am happy in my work. Writers grump about the loneliness of their task, but I suspect they secretly relish their time alone. They cherish, too, those moments when they get it right, when they find themselves in what basketball players call "the zone." Every word comes out roundly, perfectly. The rhythms of our sentences sing back at us. We have, what is called, a good day. Of course we know we'll pay for it tomorrow.

W.O. MITCHELL

W.O. MITCHELL is fondly remembered as the wild-haired raconteur of Prairie fiction. Despite his success as an author, he remained grateful for the encouragement he received as a fledgling writer and continued to offer similar support to those who came after him. He viewed it a great gift, privilege and duty to share his art with new authors as well as his readers.

The practice of all the arts is acrobatic, not much different from being a high-wire walker, a trapeze artist. No guarantee each time that you won't lose your balance and fall. And like most artists I have had spotters. Several. My first had been in high school: Miss Emily. Then Rupert Lodge here at the University of Manitoba. And years later at the University of Alberta, Professor F.M. Salter. During the first two years of writing *Who Has Seen the Wind* he was there to catch me. I owe them all.

It was during those years with Salter that I accidentally made my greatest discovery. At some point I stopped typing and leaned back to remember—not to write. Unbidden, my father, who had died when I was seven, came back to me. I remembered his reciting "In Flanders Fields"—"The Flag"—"Mr. Dooley Says"—"When Father Rode the Goat." I also remember standing with him in front of the upstairs toilet. We called it "crossing streams"—of course Mother never knew about it.

Each spring the McLaughlin seven-passenger car would come down off the blocks. Mother would take me and my brothers out to the cemetery just south of town, where we would play tag, making sure we cleared the graves, not setting a foot down on the earth mound over mortal remains. On our second or third first spring Sunday visit, there was a gopher hole right in front of the gravestone that hadn't been there the fall before. I was outraged. The gopher popped up and squeaked. He had no damn right to trespass on my dad's grave! I looked up to my mother, saw the prairie wind had laid a long dark lock of her hair across the side of her face, where tears were streaming down her cheeks.

More and more often I found myself travelling back into my stored past to find someone I had loved or hated, dramatic incidents, sights, sounds, feelings, smells. I wrote them down in detail. It wasn't writing; it was finding. When I would touch base with Salter almost weekly I would give them to him to read. In a way it was an imposition, for I was not enrolled in his creative writing class. We often met in his backyard after he had put aside the lawn mower or the hoe—or in his living room or his office at the university. At the end of almost six months in one of our meetings he said, "Bill, this stuff you've been showing me is autobiographical chaos. You've got to start behaving. I've been going over all of it to see if there's any possible literary order suggested."

He pulled the great pile of papers across his desk. With Scotch tape tabs he had singled out page parts. "Let's consider these." We went through them all one by one. The first had been the time Ike Parsons and Jack Andrews and I had discovered the pigeon nest in the loft of an abandoned barn out on the prairie. One of the eggs had just hatched out. I took the baby chick home with me, cuddled it in a handkerchief on my bedside table. Three days later it was dead. Next came the time my mother let me have a fox terrier puppy I named Tom—her suggestion because she had always regretted she had not named one of her four sons Tom. He existed just two years till the day that Snelgroves's Bakery wagon rolled over him. Then there was the two-headed calf in Stinchcombe's Livery Stable and veterinary building. I saw it the same day Mackenzie King visited our town and spoke to all the Haig School students. I ran home and shouted the exciting news to my mother and Grandma and Aunt Josie: "I've seen everything! The Prime Minister of Canada and a two-headed calf!" Next came the day of my father's funeral in our living room with the open casket in front of our fireplace. There was the birth of my youngest brother, Dickie, when I was four. The death of my grandmother.

Salter shoved the papers aside. "Do you notice anything promising in the way of a novel?"

"I don't know."

"Consider. First there's the just-born baby pigeon … then its death. Then there's the puppy, then he dies. Your father's funeral, the two-headed calf, your brother's birth, your grandmother's death. Get it?"

"No."

"Birth, then death, then birth, then death?"

"I don't know."

"It's a clear pattern. Could suggest a possible novel."

"Still don't get it. No plot."

"Forget plot. Think symphony."

"Whaaaat?!"

"Alternating high and low notes."

"Sheeyit! I was born tone-deaf!"

"There are notes of vulgarity too. Look Bill, all art is one and indivisible." Whatever that meant. "Take a run at it."

I did. The result five years later was my first published novel: *Who Has Seen the Wind*. How I owe that man and the others—but especially him. In time I came to understand what he meant when he said, "All art is one and indivisible." He persuaded me to forget law study and become a teacher. After I got my certificate I taught officially as a high school principal for only two years. But ever since then I have helped writing protégés as a teacher and as an artist in residence in five different universities and at the Banff School of Fine Arts. I had no choice—I had to discharge my gratitude debt to Miss Emily and Lodge and Salter. It had been one hell of a creative breakthrough Salter had given me. Many of us in what Margaret Laurence referred to as "the tribe" have been helping first writers. Is any experience more satisfying than seeing their success?

Death and solitude justify art, which draws human aliens together in the mortal family, uniting them against the heart of darkness. Humans must comfort each other, defend each other against the terror of being human. Thus the dictum of Conrad (another existentialist), "We exist only in so far as we hang together—woe to the stragglers." Humans must comfort one another, defend each other against the terror of being human. There is a civilized accountability to others. The coyote, the jackrabbit, the badger, the killdeer, the weasel, the undertaker beetle, do not have that accountability. As a child I never did run across an artistic gopher or weasel or badger—though I'm not so certain about dragonflies or meadow larks. Coyotes and ants are quite political. The wolf is very much aware of territorial imperative.

The novelist Wallace Stegner, who was a prairie boy till he was fourteen in Eastend, Saskatchewan, has said in his book *Wolf Willow* that the prairie creates poets. I agree—all that land and all that sky do make poets. Prairie certainly teaches early that to be human means to be conscious of self—and separation from the rest of the living whole. "Human" therefore equals "lonely." Stegner used the word, poet, in the sense of its Greek origin—"maker." All artists make or create and the result is an important ingredient in the recipe for culture, for those bridges and patterns which connect us, which create human "solidarity." Humans are the only animals who make poems, plays, novels; the only animals who paint, dance, sing, sculpt, compose. Artists, philosophers, historians know that man is a finite, warm sack of vulnerability. And because of this knowledge they do have an unfair advantage over politicians—generals—and quarterbacks—and CEOs. Art is the only thing that man does for its own sake, that does not involve an adversary relationship. There are no winners over losers, no victors over vanquished, no toreador over bull. Readers are creative partners. As they read they have explosions of recognition from their own experience—somebody they have loved or hated, sensuous fragments, insights. Instead of relying entirely on what is written, they contribute from their own unique past, thereby making the fictional illusion all the more vivid and meaningful. Creative partners to artists, who look and wonder at a painting or a play or a ballet, who listen to a symphony—or even an opera—do not take anything from the artist. The book is not taken from the author. Both partner and artist win—through shared pity and terror, compassion and empathy, laughter and tears.

The writer explores and reveals bridges and patterns to the human community. They are fragile and they can be destroyed. They are only man-made. They are not divine, or absolute; they are life patterns, which grow like life and which change in a living manner. Man has grown them out of his generation after generation flow to defeat the heart of darkness. Exploring these patterns and bridges is of particular importance to our young. Our vulnerable young.

Many years ago Socrates said that the unexamined life was not worth living. Now, there's an old prairie expression that says much the same thing: "Don't you eat that there stuff, Elmer. It's bull shit." But humans do not live by reason and common sense alone—neither the simply intellectual life nor the purely utilitarian life is the whole answer. We must have *artistic* life as well. Over a hundred and seventy years ago, Shelley wrote, "We have more moral, political, and historical wisdom than we know how to reduce into practice. There is no want of knowledge respecting what is wise and best in morals, government, and political economy. We want the poetry of life. Poets are the unacknowledged legislators of the world."

Shelley's warning—that our utilitarian culture has eaten more than it can digest—is even more relevant today. Which means that our culture is in even more need of the shared gift of the writer, the "poetry of life."

II. ON INTRIGUING CHARACTERS

GRANT MACEWAN

Professor of Agriculture, Alderman and Mayor of Calgary, and Lieutenant Governor of Alberta, GRANT MACEWAN still found time to pen numerous books of local history. His forte was bringing to life fascinating personages from our recent and distant past. Bob Edwards was so good at this, some folks thought his fictional characters were real.

Grant MacEwan

As pioneers with good memories will agree, he was one of Western Canada's fabulous personalities—Peter J. McGonigle. In the period after 1905 when the provinces of Saskatchewan and Alberta were created, he ranked among the best known citizens in the prairie country. Folk who gathered at the livery stables talked about Peter McGonigle. Nearly everybody read about him, following his fortunes and misfortunes with as much interest as is now shown in favorite hockey teams. His behavior was not always exemplary although that did not seem to affect his following and popularity.

But while nearly everybody read about Peter McGonigle, nobody saw him in the flesh. The fact was that Peter never actually lived. He was a mythical character created by that equally amazing person, Bob Edwards, editor of the Calgary Eye Opener.

Even today, however, there need be no apology for treating Peter J. McGonigle, Esquire, as though he were as real as Bob Edwards made him appear, and following the poor soul through some of the tribulations that made him famous and some that proved a threat to the calm of Empire relations in his time.

For the purpose of the record, Peter McGonigle was an editor. Yes, he presided over the Midnapore Gazette and wrote the "Society Notes" and other ribald features for the miniature metropolis of Midnapore—a few miles south of Calgary—with a master hand. But an editor must be a man of many parts and Peter was versatile, having several sidelines including bootlegging and horse stealing.

The sidelines being more profitable than editorship, took more of his time and contributed more generally to his fame. But whatever may have been his status on the voters' list, McGonigle and the Eye Opener accounts of his escapades brought more publicity to his alleged village of Midnapore than the most active chamber of commerce could have done.

Years after both Peter McGonigle and his creator, Bob Edwards, had passed from the local scene, a handsome car bearing an American license, stopped at Midnapore while the driver enquired if any members of the Peter McGonigle family were still living thereabout. Unfortunately, there was no McGonigle to whom one could point but, surely, the ghost of the inimitable Peter still hovers about the village.

Peter McGonigle's first publicity was through the Eye Opener of August 22, 1903, while that paper was being published at High River. Thereafter, Peter was drunk quite frequently, sometimes went to jail but, always, he was cheerful. Often he was the hero in Bob Edwards' fiction and, now and then, he'd lend his name to a local story of fact when it was considered prudent to hide the identity of the real participant.

Notwithstanding his obvious talent in some lines of endeavor, he seemed to be born for misfortune; even his romances were fraught with peril. One of those affairs, as reported by Bob Edwards, followed Peter's decision to lead a better life. He joined the village church and, having a voice far louder than a foghorn on a Mississippi river-boat, there was an immediate demand that he become part of the church choir. Being an agreeable fellow, our Peter accepted the assignment affably and, the very first Sunday, according to the Eye Opener report, distinguished himself by nearly "shattering the Rock of Ages into a thousand fragments."

That, however, was beside the point. More important, there was a pretty young widow singing contralto and Peter was attracted. By the second Sunday, Peter and the widow were singing from the same hymn-book. Now, it must be explained that at this particular period in his career, when he wasn't writing copy for the Midnapore Gazette, he was turning an honest penny by selling sewing machines.

One evening, he decided that to try selling a machine to the widow would provide an excellent excuse for calling. Accordingly, between eight and nine o'clock, accompanied by his faithful dog, he knocked at the front door of the lady's residence. The greeting was cordial and, on being admitted, Peter ordered the little dog to lie down on the porch to wait for him.

When this enthusiastic editor-turned-salesman was explaining the merits of the sewing machine, the dog sprang from the porch to run after a passing buggy and during the five minutes or so when the animal was absent, Peter McGonigle took his departure. He meandered down to the hotel but finding the bar closed, he went to bed, wondering hazily what had become of the dog.

What he didn't know about the dog was that after chasing a horse-drawn rig down the trail leading to Okotoks, the animal returned to the porch of the widow's cottage to await its master, not knowing that McGonigle had gone home. Faithful dog that McGonigle owned, the brute was still there in the morning when some of the Midnapore citizens going to work at an early hour, saw him lying asleep at the widow's front door and drew their own conclusions. It wasn't a nice situation.

By ten o'clock, everybody in Midnapore had heard about it and poor Peter— his explanations were all in vain. An officer of the church called at the office of the Gazette and asked Peter to refrain from returning to the choir. The unfortunate lady moved to the East where she wouldn't be haunted by reproachful glances and the unhappy McGonigle threatened to move his publishing business to some place like Okotoks or Dundurn.

But nothing in the McGonigle career brought as much notoriety to either himself or Bob Edwards as the printed account of the Calgary banquet tendered to McGonigle on the occasion of his release from penitentiary where he had been serving time for horse stealing. The echos from that famous reception were heard round the world. The spark that "fired the heather" was the report concerning the banquet, appearing in the columns of the Calgary Eye Opener on October 6, 1906.

The report made it clear that the fine affair, tendered by the Calgary Board of Trade to honor Peter McGonigle on the occasion of release from Edmonton penitentiary, was a huge success. Many prominent citizens were present and Calgary's Mayor Emerson occupied the chair. Letters of regret were read from Lord Strathcona, Earl Grey, Premier Rutherford, Charles Wagner, Joseph Seagram, Josh Calloway and others of similar prominence.

Joseph Seagram wrote: "Dear Mr. Mayor: Though unable to be with you in the flesh, my spirit is no doubt with you in sufficient quantities. Wishing Mr. McGonigle all luck in his next venture. Yours truly, Joseph Seagram."

It was the Lord Strathcona letter that produced the real fireworks. It went this way: "John Emerson, Mayor, Calgary. Dear Jack, You don't mind me calling you Jack, do you old chap? I regret exceedingly that I shall be unable to attend the McGonigle banquet at Calgary, but believe me, my sympathies go out to your honored guest. The name of Peter McGonigle will ever stand high in the roll of eminent confiscators. Once, long ago, I myself came near achieving distinction when I performed some dexterous financing with the Bank of Montreal's funds. In consequence, however, of the CPR stocks going up instead of down, I wound up in the House of Lords instead of Stoney Mountain. Yours truly, Strathcona."

It was a gay banquet and toast followed hilarious toast. Finally, the guest of honor, the noble Peter J., arose to thank his many friends and explain that had it not been for the ignorance of his lawyer, he might have been acquitted because the horse he was accused of stealing was not a horse at all, but a mare. More than that, the stolen animal died shortly after the theft and it did not seem right that he should have to break so much government stone because of a dead horse.

The people from Winnipeg, through Saskatoon and Regina to Calgary read the story, chuckled as they did many times before when reading the Eye Opener, and thought no more about it. They knew Bob Edwards and thought they knew Peter McGonigle. No local person was surprised that Earl Grey, Lord Strathcona, Premier Rutherford and Joe Seagram were drawn into the story.

Farther from home, however, such a story could be misconstrued and sure enough it was. To the desk of John Williston, editor of the Toronto Evening News, came a copy of the Eye Opener and, knowing nothing of the background, this gentleman was amazed. At once he sensed international news in the account of Lord Strathcona and Earl Grey paying tribute to a notorious horse thief. Being the Canadian correspondent of a daily paper published in London, England, he at once prepared a story and cabled it to London.

Reading his morning paper over a pleasant cup of tea, somewhere outside of London, Lord Strathcona's eyes fell upon the story from Canada and, to his horror, noted he was quoted as having praised the ex-convict, McGonigle. This was preposterous and immediately the serious-minded peer phoned the editor of the London newspaper, demanding explanation. The English editor, no less puzzled, cabled Williston in Toronto, and he in turn dispatched a telegram to the Mayor of Calgary.

Mayor Emerson was able to report the story as a hoax, that the Eye Opener's editor was a humorist, trying to provide a little fun for frontier consumption, and the best thing for all concerned was to forget it. But Strathcona, his lordly dignity terribly upset, didn't wait for the explanation before cabling his lawyer friend in Calgary, Senator Lougheed, instructing legal action against the author who made him so disgustingly friendly with a ruffian like Peter McGonigle.

Senator Lougheed, along with other western people had read the story as it appeared in the Eye Opener and laughed at it, but to explain to an infuriated Lord beyond the Atlantic that it was not to be taken seriously, was almost impossible. It wasn't for some time that the noble Lord was persuaded to withdraw the charge and let Peter McGonigle and Bob Edwards have their fun.

Returning to freedom, McGonigle went about his nefarious business and continued to make news, until 1911, at least, when Eye Opener readers received the sad news that he was dead. The great editor was buried in the garden patch behind the Gazette office at Midnapore. Death can be cruel but nobody should have expected it to strike McGonigle in any ordinary sort of way. His loving widow, obsessed with a premonition that Peter might not have been really dead when they buried him—perhaps only in a coma—pestered the authorities until they granted permission to exhume the body, buried for several months. After medical tests for signs of life proved negative and the doctors confirmed death, the stubborn widow resorted to a final test of her own contriving; with the cold body supported in a sitting position, she held a glass of whiskey at the lifeless nostrils and when the fumes passed upward, the great editor opened his eyes and raised his right hand to take the glass.

For a few more years, Peter McGonigle was back on the pages of the Eye Opener but in 1920, it was announced that he was really dead. While examining an ivory-handled revolver belonging to the bartender at the Nevermore Hotel in Midnapore, the weapon went off and the bullet lodged in Peter's stomach. The injured man was removed to a hospital in Calgary where an emergency operation was performed. The operation was "highly successful" but "Mr. McGonigle's heart, storm-beaten by many a howling gale, failed to rise to the supreme call." According to Bob Edwards, the physicians were of the opinion that the rather unfortunate circumstances of his heart stopping had more than a little to do with his death.

People mourned for Peter J. McGonigle whose name was one of the most familiar in all the west, even though no more than a fictional character springing from the fertile imagination of that fascinating fellow, Bob Edwards, editor of the Calgary Eye Opener.

MORDECAI RICHLER

MORDECAI RICHLER made Jewish Montreal famous through the likes of Duddy Kravitz. In sharing his keen character studies, he bravely risks exposing a bit of himself. The best writers become intriguing personalities themselves, with much to offer on issues they are passionate about—consider Richler's staunch defence of anglophone rights in Quebec.

Mordecai Richler

On Monday, January 11, I came home from one of my long afternoon walks and Florence said, "I'm afraid I've got bad news. Brian Moore died last night." "God damn it," I said, pouring myself a stiff drink.

The last time I saw Brian was at the Booker Prize dinner in London in 1990. He had been shortlisted for the third time, me, the second. Neither of us won, but that's not the point. We stood there, I feeling foolish and uncomfortable in my tuxedo, exchanging pleasantries awkwardly, which was a damn shame, because we had been the closest of friends for many years. And I couldn't help wondering if Brian, like me, thought how incongruous it was that we were both posturing there, now two literary geezers, contenders, when once we had been a couple of all but inseparable provincial musketeers (no, three, counting our mutual friend Bill Weintraub), hopeful Montreal scribblers, much given to late-night revels and ridicule of what we adjudged as second-rate. Coming out of different parts of the forest, Brian and I were unstintingly supportive of each other in those days, halcyon days.

Mavis Gallant first introduced us in Paris in 1951. I was living there at the time, a college dropout, and Brian, his wife Jackie Sirois, and Bill were over on a visit. Brian and Bill were still Montreal *Gazette* reporters, Jackie was working for *Weekend* magazine, and I, who would go on to publish too early, was struggling with what would turn out to be a derivative first novel. We drank into the early morning hours at the Deux Magots, testing each other with feelers. Brian, shocked that I had not yet read *Ulysses*, I delighted that he was familiar with Isaac Babel's short stories. Discovering we shared a mutual regard for Waugh and Nathanael West. There was an immediate rapport.

On my return to Montreal in 1953 I began to see a good deal of the Moores and Weintraub. Brian had quit the *Gazette* and was churning out Gold Medal paperback thrillers under a pseudonym, something he later became touchy about, which was unnecessary. A writer responsible for so many fine novels, never repeating himself, his range astonishing, had no reason to apologize any more than Salinger had for writing *Saturday Evening Post* stories to begin with, or Rushdie for once having worked for an ad agency. We all have to pay the rent.

Brian and I helped each other. I introduced him to Diana Athill, my editor at Andre Deutsch, and she took on *The Lonely Passion of Judith Hearne*, which announced the emergence of a large talent. I once teased Brian about that. "You made a mistake, publishing such a grand first novel. Me, after *The Acrobats*, I could only get better. But you are in trouble."

Later Brian spoke to his American publisher, Seymour Lawrence of Atlantic Monthly Press, on my behalf, and Sam published *The Apprenticeship of Duddy Kravitz*. The flamboyant Sam, who was given to stammering when troubled, was something of an enigma to Brian and another one of his then authors, Herbert Gold. Is Sam Jewish, they wanted to know? I'll ask him, I said. So one evening as Florence, Sam, and I sat in a London taxi, bound for a restaurant, I dropped the sandbag. "Are you Jewish, Sam?"

"H-h-h-half," he allowed, and I immediately reported to Brian, because that was the kind of story we enjoyed sharing.

The pleasures of his company were immense. He was witty, acerbic, and a splendid raconteur, but the obituary writers who described him as modest got it wrong. Brian did not indulge in advertisements for himself. He was not a braggart or self-promoter, but neither was he modest. He had a sense of his own worth, and why not? Unlike me, generous to a fault, he could also be touchy, difficult, and scathing about other writers. He had strong opinions. Rigorous standards.

We continued to see a good deal of each other in Montreal, London, the Alpes-Maritimes, and one memorable summer out on Long Island. Nineteen sixty-two that was, and Brian and Jackie, regulars in Amagansett, found us a house there, and as we knew nobody, introduced us around, made sure we were invited to parties. Florence and I had three small children at the time: Daniel, Noah, and Emma. Daniel and the Moores' son Michael played together. Brian taught Daniel how to ride a two-wheel bicycle. He was Emma's godfather. Bill Weintraub drove down to spend a weekend with us and stayed on for six or seven weeks. Mornings at the post office Brian and I would be pissed off by Neil "Doc" Simon, who, unfailingly, fished a huge mound of mail out of his box, while we had to make do with only a humiliating letter or two. One morning TV playwright David Shaw, Brian, and I hired a boat out of Montauk and went shark fishing together. The rough-hewn captain of our vessel, we agreed, was a real man, not a bookish ninny like the rest of us, but we were proved wrong. "You guys writers?" he asked.

Yes, we confessed, caught out, as it were.

So he descended into his cabin and emerged again with fifty-odd pages of manuscript. "Would you read this, please?"

In different countries much of the time, Brian and I regularly exchanged jokey, irreverent letters. Once, when Florence and I were in Los Angeles, long after Brian and Jackie had divorced, Brian and Jean, his second wife, were good enough to throw a party for us at their home in Malibu. It was obvious they were very happy together.

Then, unhappily, there was a rupture in our friendship. There was no quarrel. We simply drifted apart. Brian, I heard, thought it was improper of me to have joined the judges' panel at the Book-of-the-Month Club, pronouncing on other writers' work. And I countered by wondering how he could teach the unteachable, creative writing, at the University of California. If we met, it was now at public occasions. A panel in Toronto on Novels into Film; Brian, David Cronenberg, and me. Or pausing briefly to greet each other in a hotel lobby when we were both reading on different nights at Harbourfront, and then moving on to separate dinner parties.

In a resoundingly misinformed review of Denis Sampson's book, *Brian Moore: The Chameleon Novelist*, Dennis Duffy wrote in *The Globe and Mail* about Brian's battle with the bottle, suggesting that he was once an alcoholic. I hope Brian was amused rather than angered by such nonsense. Of course he drank. We all did. But he was too disciplined and prolific a novelist to have ever been a drunk.

Brian once said, "Canadians are obviously not quite sure I'm a Canadian writer, and the Americans have never accepted me as anything other than a foreigner."

His international reputation huge, it seems to me that Brian never got his due in Canada. Neither McGill nor the University of Toronto awarded him an honourary degree, and he was never appointed to the Order of Canada, obviously adjudged less distinguished than some of the most recent recipients: say, Irving Pink, Yarmouth, N.S., lawyer; or Sally Armstrong, Oakville, Ont., mass media; or Jacqueline Desmarais, Montreal, arts. (Jacqueline Desmarais, arts? If that's the case, why not Don Cherry, ideas?)

The last time I heard from Brian was when I was in the hospital last summer for some unpleasant surgery. It was a note wishing me well, and, in my vulnerable state, I shed a few tears for our foolishly aborted friendship. In my mind's eye, I keep going back to the night of that Booker Prize dinner, the two of us, stuffed into tuxedos, too boyishly proud to make a first move, mending matters. And Florence and Jean, who were both more sensible, and knew better, were obviously rendered helpless by their loyalties. And now it is too late.

Fortunately, it is not my place to put Brian's work on the scales and pronounce on its weight. Time alone will settle that, and time is an unreliable bitch. Who now reads William Sansom's novels, which I still hold in high regard? Or James T. Farrell's Studs Lonigan trilogy? Or Ring Lardner's short stories? Or the underestimated Julian McLaren-Ross? All the same, without making too large a claim for a departed old friend, W.H. Auden's lines on the death of Yeats keep ricocheting through my head. To paraphrase:

"Earth, receive an honoured guest;
Brian Moore is laid to rest."

PETER C. NEWMAN

An astute observer of literary, economic and political affairs, PETER NEWMAN
offers insightful studies of people and events. Newman is one of countless
Canadians with non-Canadian roots, a refugee background, or other
international connections who widen the perspective of Canadian journalism.
Increased credibility comes with first-hand knowledge of any subject.

I only met him once, but I've never forgotten my few private moments with
Vaclav Havel, the secular saint who last week fell critically ill in Prague and,
according to his doctors, may not recover.

Our brief meeting took place in Ottawa in 1990, when he was on his way to
Washington to address a joint session of Congress, and he didn't have much time.
But he was glad to meet someone who could speak Czech, so he wouldn't have to
rely on his interpreter. (She was a tiny Oriental woman he kept tucked under his left
shoulder, who was so good at her job that as local well-wishers talked to him, she
would whisper to Havel in Czech, lip read his answer and reply almost instanta-
neously in perfect Oxford English.)

From our brief exchange, I recall only two fragments. "I've learned never to be
surprised by anything," he shrugged, when I asked how it felt for a beleaguered playwright to suddenly find himself a famous president. To my question about the secret
of politics, he shot back: "Write your own speeches and express hard truths in a
polite way." Then he paused, and added: "Of course, everyone is replaceable."

I'm not so sure.

Havel was one of those rare conscience-driven politicians we can't afford to lose. He kept himself removed from the darker tricks of his craft and was never impressed by the fumes of fame. Havel believed that character is destiny and that it was therefore essential to live a principled life, even at the risk of being imprisoned for his beliefs—which he was.

A scruffy man with originally ginger-colored hair and an orange moustache (one friend joked, "Vaclav looks as if carrot juice is flowing through his veins"), he enjoyed a highly developed sense of the absurd. His plays were absurdist creations in mundane settings with universal characters. Havel started writing when he was 13, but Czech theatre was closed to him until the Velvet Revolution of 1989.

He led the peaceful overthrow of the occupying Russians and in the winter of 1989 assumed Czechoslovakia's presidency. That meant moving into Hradcany Castle, a huge pile of palaces and cathedrals overlooking the Vltava River, which bisects Prague. Just eight months earlier, he had been serving a four-year sentence in a communist prison a few kilometres away.

He had been the spiritual catalyst of the bloodless revolt that swept the Communists out of power, and now he was the country's first democratic president since 1938. Being a playwright, one of the first things Havel did was to make sure everyone wore appropriate costumes. He asked his friend Theodor Pistek (who won an Academy Award for his costumes in the movie Amadeus) to design properly pretentious royal blue parade uniforms—complete with toy sabres—for the castle guards. When they were delivered, Havel tried one on, and yelling, "Let's go scare the cooks!" ran into the castle kitchens, waving his pretend weapon. He later got fed up with soldiers marching around the castle to regal marching music and had one of his friends compose a jarring melody in seven-eighths time that no one could possibly march to, then insisted it be played for the changing of the guard ceremonies. Hradcany Castle is so huge that Havel sometimes resorted to getting around the place on a scooter, and after the first few weeks in office he agreed not to come to work in jeans and received visitors wearing a polka-dot tie. (His first press secretary was Michael Zantovsky, whose only claim to fame was as the author of the only study in Czech of the films of Woody Allen.)

As president (he was re-elected in 1990 and 1993), Havel granted amnesty to 30,000 prisoners, presided over the peaceful withdrawal of Soviet troops, defied public opinion by supporting the reunification of Germany, masterminded the Czech Republic's NATO application, and brought some badly needed enlightenment to a country that had not known democracy since 1938.

But his main contributions were his evocative speeches, written by himself on a manual typewriter. Probably the best was his 1990 New Year's message: "For 40 years, on this day, you heard the same thing in different variations from my predecessors: how our country flourishes, how many tons of steel we produced, how happy we all are, how we trust our government and what bright perspectives were unfolding in front of us. I assume you did not nominate me to this office so that I, too, would lie to you. Our country is not flourishing. Entire branches of industry are producing goods that are of no interest to anyone. A country that once could be proud of the educational level of its citizens spends so little on education that it ranks today as 72nd in the world."

He went on like that for about ten minutes, then came his seminal point: "Let us teach both ourselves and others that politics does not have to be the art of the possible, especially if this means the art of intrigues, secret agreements and pragmatic manoeuvrings. But that it can also be the art of the impossible, that is the art of making both ourselves and the world better."

"Man," Havel once wrote from jail, "is nailed down—like Christ on the cross—to a grid of paradoxes. He balances between the torment of not knowing his mission and the joy of carrying it out."

Vaclav Havel did both. We were all the better for it, and if his current illness claims him, we shall mightily miss his impish presence.

JUNE CALLWOOD

JUNE CALLWOOD is a crusader, a socially aware individual who acts on her strong beliefs. Achieving impressive practical results for sometimes controversial causes, Callwood also applauds everyone who uses their special gifts and energies to ensure that the underdog has an effective voice.

Bob Edwards' closest match in Toronto is Mendelson Joe, an artist and pleasant man who is approaching the top end of middle-age in a state of unadulterated outrage, which he markets as comedy. I think Bob Edwards would have liked him a lot.

Mendelson Joe, unbundled against the December cold in tattered shorts, a sweater, paint-splattered sneakers and a yellow cap with bunny ears flopping on his forehead, last Sunday staged a protest against Bill C-54 in front of Toronto's Art Gallery of Ontario, attracting the attention of several people.

His was not intended as the definitive protest against the federal government's anti-pornography bill to amend the Criminal Code. Larger events are afoot. Tomorrow, for instance, Toronto's public libraries will close in order to draw attention to the costs to libraries of reclassifying their books so that people under eighteen can't read about sex. Museums, theatres and art galleries are planning "To Be Banned" exhibits and a national day of protest is under consideration.

Mendelson Joe's statement was on a smaller scale: one big, sweet-natured man in bunny ears alone against the frigid elements of Canadian winter and Canadian prudery, treating them with equal disdain.

Suspended from his massive shoulders was his declaration on censorship, a giant postcard addressed to Justice Minister Ramon Hnatyshyn expressing Mendelson Joe's view that C-54 will interfere with his rights, as an artist, to "depict consenting adults in various kinds of loving intercourse."

Mendelson Joe, 43 years old, robust and benign, is a self-taught painter, composer and guitarist who has been famous, intermittently, for each of his accomplishments. He's an artist who has had an acclaimed one-man show in Paris and whose works hang in the homes of such collectors as writer-actor Don Harron, and a musician whose albums have had a cult following in Canada for several years, and whose bluesy-rock group, Mainline, was a success in England.

One of his best known songs is *I Think I'm Losing My Marbles*. The record could be purchased at most outlets during the 1970s, or people could descend to the platforms of Toronto subways and hear the sunny composer singing it himself.

As a painter, he places himself in the forefront of the Dauntless Evidentist Movement. He is, in fact, the only member of that movement. The name was invented by friends, a lawyer and an art consultant, who based it on the certifiable truth that Mendelson Joe is dauntless and also on their observation that his paintings contain no tricks: everything they are about is evident. Mendelson Joe once painted a potato that looks exactly like a potato. It floats serenely against a solid blue background, which transforms the composition. What the spectator can perceive with ease is that this is a portrait of a sky-borne potato. The message respectfully is omitted. I own it.

Mendelson Joe's imagination wears springs. He has an innocent way with a sentence. He says: "Art to some people is just a nickname for Arthur" and "The name of the game ain't schmaltz, it's results" and "Whenever I'm away from Canada the thing I miss most is the apathy" and "I do not own a Mercedes Benz car, but I can play the guitar."

He is regarded by some as a crazy who is drawn to serious causes, and by others as a man of profoundly serious intent who wears craziness as a loss leader to get people in the store. Last Sunday he had a rational explanation for the bunny hat. He said he wanted to attract attention to his protest and a big man in bunny ears is a more arresting sight than the same man in a fedora.

He resists efforts to categorize him as an eccentric. He sees himself as a normal, healthy, sane man. It's the militant conformists who are the true eccentrics. He declares that Sinclair Stevens (former federal industry minister) is very eccentric. Mendelson Joe thinks it is eccentric to allow violence on television but ban depictions of love-making. He thinks it is eccentric to abuse people or poison a lake.

His paintings are bright acrylics on large canvasses. He'll paint anything—barnyards, erotica, his mother, landscapes, still life, bunnies, jokers, smokers, a storm of guitars falling from the sky, portraits of prime ministers whose faces are reshaped to resemble backsides. His output is about three hundred paintings a year. Consequently there are thousands of Mendelson Joe originals stashed in warehouses and hundreds more piled in his studio, awaiting customers.

He supports himself entirely from the sale of his paintings and adjusts his prices to suit his clients' pocketbooks. Stan Joskowitz, who works in the post office, is in the process of acquiring one for $20 a month. Very frequently, Mendelson Joe gives his paintings away. Both Pollution Probe and the International Institute of Concern for Public Health have Mendelson Joe paintings which are given free to people who donate $1,000 or more.

Mendelson Joe comes from a sensible family that does not know quite what to make of him. He cannot figure them out either. He wonders why they are not more upset by what is happening to the environment.

He started to play the guitar at eleven and decided he was a musician. Then he went to the University of Toronto and acquired a BA despite confining his academic pursuits to football and women. Midway in a flourishing career as a musician, he signed a recording contract that described him as an artist. Impressed, he decided to paint.

He was born Birrell Josef Mendelson but in 1975 he started experimenting with new names. The first one he chose was Elvis Mendelson, but it did not do as much for his career as he had hoped, so he dropped it. He tried fourteen names before deciding that Mendelson Joe is perfect.

Next Sunday he might be back in front of the art gallery to continue his protest against Bill C-54. He could be wearing the bunny hat, but maybe not. He thinks Canadians do not have a really good sense of humour.

PETER GZOWSKI

PETER GZOWSKI must surely have one of Canada's most widely recognised voices. Entering homes across the country each morning, he reverently introduced Canadians to their literary heroes, from aspiring to well-established. Gzowski became an important thread strengthening the Canadian literary fabric.

My only regret in all the chats I had with Robertson Davies over the years is that I never did figure out what to call him. Rob? I couldn't bring myself to say it. Dr. Davies? I suppose so. Maybe just ... the Master.

PETER GZOWSKI Robertson Davies is internationally respected as one of Canada's leading men of letters, and his productivity has been undeterred by age. At eighty-one he has just published his eleventh novel, called *The Cunning Man*, and in typical Davies fashion, it covers a variety of subjects, including, in this case, medicine, cannibalism, and Shakespeare's constipation. Robertson Davies is with me now. Good morning, sir.

ROBERTSON DAVIES Good morning, good morning.

PG I thought you were going to quit. I thought when *Murther and Walking Spirits* came out in 1991, you said that was the end.

RD Well, I know I said that, but the habits of a lifetime are not easily broken, and what would I do if I didn't go on?

PG Well, some of the characters from *Murther and Walking Spirits* appear in *The Cunning Man*.

RD Yes.

PG So does Dunstan Ramsay from *Fifth Business*.

RD That's right.

PG I wonder if some of these people have taken over your life.

RD Well, it could be, but I wouldn't be a good judge of that.

PG But do they have lives of their own? Do they exist for you?

RD In a sense, yes, but I'm hesitant to talk about that kind of thing because some authors are so pretentious about their characters, as though they were real people whom they had mysteriously brought into the world. And that's pushing it a little far.

PG You mean you made them up?

RD I made them up out of my own head. And, as we used to say when I was a schoolboy, lots of wood left.

PG You set a lot of your fiction in Toronto, but *The Cunning Man* is really almost a history of the artistic and religious elements of *this* place and *that* time of the postwar city. Is that a city that's gone?

RD Not entirely. It's a city that's changed radically, but it was a very, very interesting change. And I have been fortunate in having a chance to watch it. I came here to be a schoolboy when I was fourteen, and had a chance to see the city as it was then. And I've been watching it ever since. And the change has been fantastic. From, really a kind of colonial place to a great big international, metropolitan city.

PG What about the change of values, though? The values of the time that you write about in *The Cunning Man*, the church defines many of them, the connection with Empire defines many of them. Have the values gone?

RD Oh, yes, they have. History outside Canada has conditioned that. You couldn't have that gigantic 1939-45 war and the subsequent decline in prestige of Great Britain and that sort of thing without it affecting Canada. And also what goes on in the United States affects us a good deal. And history has a great part, well, everything to do with making Canada what it is today.

PG What about the changing nature of Canada itself and the way we think about it? Your hero, Jonathan Hullah, talks about our preoccupation with sincerity. He deplores that because he thinks it strips life of beauty. Has that changed?

RD No. It used to be very much so that a Canadian was regarded as a sort of Honest John, whom you would trust with anything. We still cherish that and cherish a kind of myth of innocence and sincerity—which is a myth, but it's our myth. It's not like the American myth, which is the myth of success, and the clever guy, and the fellow who makes it big in the world. We don't have that quite so much. We tend more to the sincere, good, honest, decent person whose word is his bond. And of course that is very far from being the picture of a typical Canadian, but it's the one we cherish. You see, we have the reputation of being great international peacekeepers. And that is a good reputation to have. But we don't want to have with it the reputation of Mr. Good Guy, you know, who can always be called upon to rush with bandages and a peanut butter sandwich whenever anyone's in trouble.

PG Do you sense a certain hypocrisy in the way we proclaim our own virtuousness and don't always act virtuously?

RD Any virtue that is proclaimed is bound to be hypocritical.

PG Did you just make that up?

RD No, well, I didn't. It's just the truth.

PG No, but it sounds as if it should be in *Bartlett* or something.

RD Well, I don't know.

PG It will be.

RD This self-regarding sincerity is bound to be somewhat hypocritical. It is insincere to think about your own sincerity, if you follow what I mean.

PG But if you can fake sincerity you have it made, as people say. What about your fascination with the word "cunning," as in *The Cunning Man.*

RD Well, that is an expression that used to be, and may still be, somewhat current in the remoter parts of rural Great Britain. The cunning man I can remember from when I was a boy and used to visit my father's place in Wales; there were cunning men in the district, and cunning women, too. The cunning women and the cunning men were people who would help you with illnesses. The cunning man was sometimes a bone-setter. He was sometimes a horse doctor. But he was also somebody who might help you to find lost objects, or he might help you if your herd was beginning to look rather peaky. He might tell you someone had put a spell on it, and that he would take the spell off. And if you wanted to put a spell on your neighbour's flock maybe he could be persuaded to do that, too. He was a kind of person people consulted, as I think nowadays city people consult psychoanalysts and the people they call counsellors—people who are supposed to know more than the rest of us.

PG So when did Jonathan Hullah begin to take shape in the way you've described him, both metaphorically and really.

RD Oh, I've been thinking about him for a very long time. And thinking about cunning men and their place in the modern world, because, well, he is a modern cunning man. The old cunning men in the seventeenth century were sort of country wizards.

PG Wizards? Wizards appeal to you?

RD Well, yes. People think of a wizard as a fellow who goes around in a cloak and casts spells all the time. Not necessarily so. He may be just somebody who knows a lot of things that the rest of the neighbourhood doesn't know. He knows who may have committed a robbery, he knows who may have got a girl into trouble and who isn't admitting it. He knows all kinds of things that aren't general knowledge. Maybe a cunning man nowadays might go into journalism. I don't know.

PG Can I ask you a little bit about journalism? This is, in a sense, a digression. One of the premises of the book—one of the devices of the book is to have a younger journalist exploring Dr. Hullah's mind and looking at his life.

RD Yes.

PG And he muses about whether it's—and this is the theme of the whole book in many ways—he muses about whether she, or anyone, can ever capture truth.

RD Exactly. And I don't believe they can. Any experienced judge or courtroom lawyer will tell you how extraordinarily varied the evidence may be which a whole lot of obviously quite honest people give about a certain incident. They all see, for instance, an accident in a rather different way.

PG I don't know if you ever took that undergraduate psychology course which would begin—they would have an unexpected event in front of the class. Someone would fake a shooting or something, then they'd have various people recount what they'd seen, and they'd all be different.

RD Yes.

PG When were you conscious of the limitations of journalism? When you were a young journalist?

RD Oh, yes. You see, I grew up in a family that were all journalists. All my family were in the history of the business. And we were very well aware of the fact that although we did the best we could, as honestly as we could, we weren't uttering final truths. How were you going to find that out? Often you did find out something—long after it had been reported and had vanished from the public consciousness—that offered a whole perspective on what had happened.

PG You must have been a very good young journalist, because I didn't know that. When I was a young journalist I thought I was writing truth and then entering it in the daily press every day. Maybe not truth, but accuracy, which is probably not always the same thing. But I was quite sure then, and later—certainly as a magazine writer, I had the conceit that a magazine profile could actually summarize somebody or tell the truth about them.

RD I don't think profiles can possibly do that even when they are extremely search-ing, because it is one person's personality sifted through another, and inevitably the sift-ing personality colours what is said. I'm very much aware when I'm interviewed by some newspaper people that what is going to appear is in actual fact a portrait of the interviewer. Because they bring with them, when they come to see me, presuppositions and ideas of what I am and what I ought to be and what I am not. And then those somehow will find their way into what they write. This is not necessarily the whole truth. In fact, I don't know how you get at the whole truth. I don't pretend to know the whole truth about myself.

PG Are novels true?

RD No, novels are creations, which are supposed to have the ring of truth. But again it is a thing which admits a second look. Now you read a very great novel, like Tolstoy's *War and Peace*. And you can think about the characters in it and get an idea of them which is entirely different from that which Tolstoy has described. And it is interesting: at the end of that book the beautiful, charming, delightful, irresistible girl Natasha is gradually getting to be a fat house-wife who wears spectacles and is pretty sharp with her husband. If you developed that you'd get a very interesting story.

* * *

PG Have you ever forgotten anything that you have experienced?

RD Not really, no. I'm not a forgetter, I'm a rememberer.

PG Is it true that banks used to spy on social gatherings in Toronto to suss out civil libertarians?

RD Why do you say *used to*? You see, this is one of the things which is important to my book, Peter. There are all kinds of people in a big city like this, where a lot of important things happen, who want information, and they get it from people who are called private investigators, or something of that kind. But they're really just snoops, gumshoe men, and they're paid usually quite substantially. The interesting thing is that the police do not pay their informers very generously. But some of the financial houses have informers, and the insurance companies, and they pay pretty well.

PG So this is a comment from the Toronto that's in the book to the world as it is now?

RD Yes. The idea that the world is full of secrets, and that you can get away with things if you just don't attract too much attention, is a great mistake. This comes from my old experience as a journalist. There are no secrets. One of the things you find out when you work on a newspaper, particularly in a moderate-sized place, as I did, is that behind every suicide was a story which you couldn't possibly tell in the paper.

PG The rules about that have changed, substantially, in our time. In some places the old rules were the better rules, about what could be said and what couldn't be said. There have even been instances in at least one paper you used to be associated with, the Kingston *Whig-Standard*.

RD Yes.

PG Are we now too ... Is your old profession or craft now too nosy? Does it have too much licence?

RD It depends entirely on the men who are controlling the paper. Sometimes they interfere and publish information which is necessary, which the public ought to know about, because it influences the public good, and it influences—as in the case that you speak of—a lot of other people, who are not able to protect themselves, very young people.

I'll tell you a tale that came within my own experience, which was about a bank manager in a moderate-size place who went out hunting. When he was alone, he had a hunting accident, and it killed him. Well, everybody knew that it was suicide. A great many people knew why. He had been getting into money which wasn't his, and he had been getting into it because he'd had to associate with men who had much more money than he had and he thought it a disadvantage. So he had set up some phony accounts and was getting money into them and using it for his own purposes. Now, his number two, his assistant manager, knew that, and he had had a great crisis of conscience. Should he inform headquarters or should he leave things alone and not be a squealer? He decided not to be a squealer. Well, when it all came out, the bank was very hard on that man. They thought he ought to have been a squealer and they punished him. They punished him quite severely. They put him in a department of his bank in which there would have been no promotion ever. Now that's the kind of way things happen that you don't hear about and that you can't publish in the papers. You can publish when an organist is abusing choirboys.

PG Ought you to?

RD Yes. I think you should, because it is a scandal which has to be brought out or else many boys will fail. In the case you spoke of, one of those boys committed suicide and two had very serious nervous breakdowns because they were not the natural prey of that kind of man. They were people who were sucked into it because they couldn't resist somebody who was in authority.

PG But if there are cases where unpalatable personal truths should be reported when the law is involved, and if there are cases where they should not be reported, who is to decide which is which? All journalists are not as wise as you and I . . .

RD No, and you have to depend on . . .

PG . . . and I'm not sure about us.

RD Well, I'm not sure about us. But you see all of that hullabaloo that went on about the Prince of Wales and that unwise telephone call or letter or something he wrote, there was no reason to blat that all out in the papers. It really didn't change anything or harm anybody. What people say in circumstances of great intimacy, sexual intimacy usually, is nobody's business but their own.

PG Even when they're Heir Apparent to the Crown?

RD Yes, yes. There is not one of us who has not said things to somebody that we were deeply involved with that we would not want to have blatted out in the papers.

PG We ought not to be so foolish as to say them on the telephone, I suppose.

RD Well, I suppose so. I was told by my father when I was very young that there was no dirtier, more corrupt press than that of Great Britain. Ours over here looks like Sunday School in comparison.

PG We're getting better.

RD Yes.

JAMES MACGREGOR

JAMES MACGREGOR and his parents immigrated from
Scotland in 1906; his age equalled that of the newly
declared Province of Alberta. Starting with the fierce winter
of '06-'07, MacGregor chronicles with wit and fondness the
range of characters who first settled the West.

They called him Old Doc Phillips. No encomium could add to the lustre of the words "Old Doc." From the most remote shack thirty-five miles away in Neerlandia they came to him, galloping all through the night. From the edge of the great muskegs up Naples way they rushed to him. From Mellowdale, Paddle River, Lunnford, and Belvedere they sought his help for a loved one labouring long in childbirth or stricken with fever. Along the trails to Dunstable, Arvilla, and Picardville, Old Doc and his driving team fought their way for years through mud or storm to the bedside of a sick mother or a wasting child. Finally there came the Spanish 'flu of 1918. Far away in Swallowhurst or Sunniebend, through blizzard and snowdrift, Old Doc rode, dozing between calls, hastening to fight it. His very presence instilled a courage that often won the battle. And when it was all over and the 'flu masks were put away and services of thanksgiving filled the country schools and churches, Old Doc had a heart attack. Only he and his wife knew that till afterwards. But he fought that off too—for a while—till that day when he was attending a patient only three miles from home and they came galloping to take Mrs.

Phillips to him. "I'm going, Carrie," was all he said; "Good-bye."

That was Old Doc Phillips—a gentleman, a profound scholar, a Christian and a lover of good horses—a short man with close-cropped grey hair, flashing eyes and the grim jaw of an Irish fighter.

Why he left a practice in Michigan, why, of all places, he came to Eastburg, why he filed on the South-East of 17, diagonally across from us, and the only quarter in the whole community considered useless, no one knows. In a pioneer community the better folk do not ask. The others, those who gossip and speculate, do not matter. That is, they didn't matter until they were stricken ill. Then they sent crying for Old Doc, and he cured them.

He must have had a Christian name, but I doubt if anyone knew it, except perhaps Dad, who was his closest neighbour and best friend. He was just Old Doc Phillips. To me he was a friend and a god. I don't think I ever had his professional help, but he did much for me. He had a library filling one side of his front room with books, and good ones. He allowed me the privilege of Scott, Dickens, Cooper, and Stevenson; and had I been able to understand them, he would have introduced me to Milton and Shakespeare, Walt Whitman and Thoreau. And ever he held before me the goal of high school some day, and perhaps even university. If he had lived, I know he would have helped financially; as it was, his inspiration, added to Mother's ardent desire and Dad's pocketbook and quiet advice, eventually gave me these advantages.

One spring evening he drove up in a new buggy and tied his smart horse to a tree. Homesteaders do not wait for the knock at the door but go out to welcome the visitor, so Dad and I met him on his way to the house. We saw a short, pleasant man, with grey hair and a close-cropped moustache. Actually he was only about forty-five, but looked much older.

It is hard for one in the city to understand the pleasure brought to a bush farmer and his family by the arrival of a polite stranger. If he will give in and stay all night, so much the greater is the boon bestowed.

That first evening with Old Doc flew by while he outlined his plans for settling amongst us.

Next morning when Dad and I walked with him through the thick bush of his quarter, he seemed more delighted than dismayed by its worthlessness. On a slight rise at the south edge of his land he decided to build his log house. He could have afforded a frame house, but something about the primitiveness of a large log house and barn appealed to him. I believe he was "getting away from it all." It was necessary to break fifteen acres within three years if he was to get title to the land. This he hired someone to do, but insisted that it be done at the corner diagonally opposite from and out of sight of his buildings. Around them only enough of the forest was despoiled to plant a small garden. He, too, loved the forest.

As soon as the house was far enough built so that one room could be lived in, Mrs. Phillips came. She was a woman of great charm and kindliness. Her rugs and furniture told of a fine home in the east. As much as Old Doc loved the place, she loathed it.

Before Doc Phillips arrived, many of the neighbours had brought their illnesses, their fractures, and their aching teeth to Dad. I guess an old soldier is supposed to know about these things. Maybe his discipline encourages trust. Yet Dad of all people had little faith in many phases of medicine. Patent medicines he despised. He swore by two remedies only—permanganate of potash for cuts, and Epsom salts for everything else. "Keep your mind easy and your bowels open," was his philosophy. With this philosophy he never spent a day in hospital in his life, except for that time when he was eighty and fell off the pig-house he was building and hurt his shoulder and head; and that time, a few years later, when the "old man's friend," pneumonia, carried him gently away.

Aching teeth were the worst plague of the pioneers. Of all ills, Dad hated them the most, for in the early days, in a moment of weakness, he had prevailed upon his friend Dr. Clare Darling, a dentist in Edmonton, to give him two pairs of forceps. Soon everyone in the country came to our place for relief from toothache, and went away spitting blood but once more looking the world in the face. When Old Doc came, Dad quietly packed the forceps away in a drawer and directed his former patients to him. Until Doc's death the forceps stayed in the drawer. By that time, however, there was a town of Westlock, and a dentist there. So I can remember only two occasions after that when these instruments were used. Mother was the patient on one of these occasions, but we will tell of that later.

The other patient was old man Shelley. Early one morning he came mumbling into the kitchen, holding his swollen face and desperately pointing far back into his cavernous mouth. The impression he conveyed was that he had not slept for two nights and was nearly demented. His face was too swollen for Dad to try the job, so, with a good slug of whisky, he sent Shelley the twelve miles to the qualified dentist in Westlock. At dusk Shelley returned, whipping his team up the road. His face was worse than ever. The dentist had absolutely refused to pull his tooth till the swelling went down. Anger and pain nearly stifled Shelley. "I don't give a damn about infection, Mac," he muttered. "You pull it. Even if I drop dead an instant later, it will be a blessing compared to this." So Dad pulled it. Shelley was too far gone in pain to mind Dad's amateurish probing. When it was out, he sat down on the steps and cried with relief. In an hour or so he set off for home, but not before the whisky he had swished around in his mouth (to kill the infection, of course) had further assuaged his pain.

In times past, many of the accident cases had been brought to Dad—or he went to them. As Doc's reputation began to spread, people from near and far came flocking to him. At first Doc's place was described as being near the MacGregor homestead, so at any hour of the day or night a man in frantic haste might gallop up to the old log shack, to be redirected along the trail past the Bear Tree. Before Doc came, men or women had been ill and had either died or got well without a physician.

One of Doc Phillips's earlier patients was Mother. At that time she was thin and desperately tired, but on a homestead you just could not give in. One day she walked down through the gap in the bush for a formal consultation with Doc. He checked her over carefully and prepared a tonic, one spoonful to be taken before each meal. Armed with her bottle of medicine, she started home, but felt so tired that soon she sat down on a roadside log. After resting a few minutes Mother went on again, but in two or three hundred yards sat down once more. This time, reasoning that, if a tonic were needed, she might as well start taking it now, she uncorked the bottle and sipped at the medicine. It was sweet, aromatic, and soothing. Almost unconsciously Mother sipped, until she was startled to discover that the bottle was drained. "Good heavens," she thought, "now I've probably killed myself." But on getting up to walk, she felt much better. She had lingered so long lapping up the tonic that Doc Phillips, who with his smart team of drivers was now on his way to make a call, over-took her. Haltingly she told him what had happened to her month's supply of tonic. At first he was incredulous. Then he slapped his leg and burst into laughter. "My goodness, woman—that stuff's full of alcohol. You're probably drunk, or soon will be." Then, reaching a spot in the trail where he could do so, he turned his team for home again. "Come on," he said, "we'll go back and get another bottle—but this time, take it with a spoon!" Then he drove her up to our old log shack.

As Doc's fame spread across the country north-west of Edmonton, his practice grew. It was noticeable, however, that his wealth did not keep pace with it. Backwoods patients have little money. The few of them that can do so, pay. Many cannot. Others never expect to pay anyway. Fortunately for Doc and the community, he had some money when he came to Eastburg. It was a good thing that his driving-horses cost little to feed, and that in those days medicines, of which he had a regular dispensary, were relatively simple and cheap; otherwise he would have gone broke. Even so, it soon became evident to Doc that he could serve better if he lived in Westlock, so he moved to town during the First War.

I'm not certain whether Doc ever took a drink of spirituous liquor in a social way. If he did drink, it was in a most abstemious manner. But he had an Irish intolerance for stupid restrictions. When, about 1917, like a black pall, prohibition lowered over the land, Doc was "agin" it.

During prohibition days the only legal way you could get a drink of whisky was by prescription from a physician. By that time doctors were becoming more common in the district, so that it was relatively easy to get a prescription—at two dollars a time, mind you. In Westlock, drug stores had half their space filled with patent medicines, while the other half was liquor. Now Old Doc, stubbornly truthful and even blunt soul that he was, declared that whisky had only an infinitesimal medicinal value. He believed, however, that, used with discretion, it had a great psychological and uplifting value, and for that reason he held stubbornly to the opinion that no man had a right to deny his neighbour the proper use of it.

Old Doc, like all other physicians, had his books of liquor prescriptions, and gave them out quite freely to those who asked for them honestly. But woe betide you if you came snivelling to him with a pretended illness, hoping to get one. Prescriptions were worth two dollars in the open market, but Doc, whose income did not exceed his expenses, in all those years of prohibition never charged for one that was honestly requested nor supplied one to any man who, in his opinion, was unfit to have it. Henry Paulson, not surprisingly, was one of his visitors. Being cautious and long-headed, Henry had laid in a stock of whisky before the plebiscite was held. "Yust in case," said he. But even that generous supply could not last for ever; eventually he had to hitch up Lars and Dagmar and set off for Westlock; and Doc, who was glad to see his old neighbour, did not have to ask what was on Henry's mind.

III. ON THE IMPORTANCE OF HONEST JOURNALISM

HUGH DEMPSEY

HUGH DEMPSEY'S commitment to the First Nations people
of Western Canada has earned him the rare distinction of
being named Honourary Chief of the Blood Tribe. His strong
portrayal of the Prairie spirit in all its guises reflects the depth
of his affinity for the heritage of the West.

Hugh a. Dempsey

Throughout Bob Edwards's career his avowed goal was justice for the common man. One of the ways he saw of achieving this was through honest government. Another method was the exposure of bunko artists and four-flushers who were victimizing small investors, and he enthusiastically attacked any elements of Canadian society which he felt were unfair to the working man.

Accordingly, he was sympathetic to the plight of prostitutes, lobbied for more relaxed divorce laws, spoke out against sweat shops and was opposed to Sunday "blue" laws. In specific instances he rose to the defence of members of the RNWMP who were being denied the rewards offered for the capture of train robber Jack Miner; he exposed real estate companies which were selling fraudulent townsite properties; he threatened to reveal the name of a Calgary dentist who was molesting young women; he exposed a well-known tailor who had fathered an illegitimate child; and he revealed that the second worst dive in Calgary was never raided because it was in a building owned by a local millionaire.

Ever since his French Riviera days, Bob Edwards had been impatient with the

English upper class and the shallowness of society life. As a result, he invented his own "society notes" which became a hilarious and racy part of the *Eye Opener*. From there he branched out into medical advice and cooking recipes—all designed to ridicule the pretentiousness of society pages in the daily newspapers.

In one issue he even implied that he had engaged a local prostitute, "a creamy-complexioned lady" to do a society column for him every week. "She says she writes copy in a tea gown and slippers." On another occasion he commented that "the society editress has begun to drink more than is good for her and has taken to laughing boisterously at pink teas." Yet everyone knew the *Eye Opener* was strictly a one-man show.

The McGillicuddy case caused Bob Edwards to become disenchanted with his sojourn in Calgary. In particular, he resented the rebuke of the jury of local citizens and came to believe that he had lost his support in the prairie city.

For these reasons, in April 1909, he set out for Toronto where he hoped to relocate the *Eye Opener*. Finding conditions unfavorable there, he looked at Montreal before deciding to settle at Port Arthur. There, with the help of his faithful advertisers from Alberta, the *Eye Opener* resumed publication, and Edwards threw himself into the turmoil of Lakehead politics. However he soon discovered that Port Arthur was no better than Toronto, so at the end of the year he moved again to Winnipeg.

This city was no stranger to Edwards, for he had a number of friends on the daily newspapers there. It was also here that he realized he could publish the *Eye Opener* anywhere; his readers and advertisers simply followed him from place to place. Still being a westerner at heart, and mellowing in his attitudes about his treatment in Calgary, Edwards decided early in 1911 to return to the stampede city for good.

He was back home and well settled when the tenth anniversary of the *Eye Opener* was celebrated. "Starting with a circulation of 250," he recalled, "the rag embarked on a wild career, full of adventure by land and booze, plunging ahead regardless of the most appalling obstacles, and finally becoming an eight-page publication with a bona-fide circulation all over the Dominion of 35,000. In sending your congratulations, pray do not enclose a bottle, as we are strictly on the Water Wagon."

Edwards's comments on booze were most appropriate, for although he was a success in the journalistic field, he never won his fight against the bottle. And the long battle was never easy. He would be sober for weeks at a time and then would suddenly disappear only to surface several days or weeks later in Vancouver or perhaps in Dr. Brett's sanitarium at Banff. In the interim the *Eye Opener* failed to appear and everyone knew that Bob Edwards was drunk again.

Yet when the moral reformers launched a drive to introduce prohibition into Alberta, Edwards fully supported them. "The *Eye Opener* has no defence to offer for the booze traffic," he told his readers. "It is a bad business; none worse. We've been there. Nobody can tell us anything about it that we don't already know and our frank opinion is that the complete abolition of strong drink would solve the problem of the world's happiness." With his active support the necessary legislation was passed and in 1916 Alberta became a dry province.

Then, just as he had supported the principle of prohibition, Edwards became an outspoken opponent of its actual implementation. He found that drinking was not halted; it simply moved from the bar into the home, and many women were now turning to booze. And even though he had been an alcoholic for years, he was appalled by the results of the new law. "God knows," he wrote, "we should be the last one to talk about other people drinking. Our own reputation as a booze artist used to be second to none, but such drinking as we did was always amongst men. In twenty years' residence in Calgary we have never had a drink in a private house, nor have we ever been to one of those drunken parties in the home that we hear so much about."

During the 1910s the fiery Bob Edwards began to mellow. The pages of the *Eye Opener* were often devoted more to sports, theatrical news, humor and the broad aspects of social reform rather than to exposés of graft, corruption and moral laxity. "We cut out the rough stuff long ago," said Edwards in 1912, "and now the paper is welcomed in hundreds and hundreds of happy homes all over the land. Only last Sunday an article which appeared in the *Eye Opener* formed the basis of a sermon preached from a local pulpit."

Now perhaps the *Eye Opener* wasn't all that innocent. Many young boys had to pay their nickels and read the off-color jokes out behind the woodshed, for the paper was still an anathema in countless Canadian homes. But its reputation as a crusader more than compensated for any loss of readership on moral grounds. And as Edwards grew older, he enjoyed the increasingly respectable role of the *Eye Opener*. On one occasion he even questioned the name of his paper. "It has often occurred to us," he said, "that the name of this paper is an unfortunate one. There is nothing dignified about the title 'Eye Opener.'" He believed that public figures hesitated to quote him because the name lacked the respectability of the more common titles as the *Herald, Graphic* and *Times*.

Bob Edwards had remained a lonely bachelor during all his years in Alberta, so his readers were surprised in 1917 when, at the age of fifty-three, he married Kate Penman, a twenty-four-year-old Scottish girl. He had met her four years earlier, just after her arrival from the old country. Working in Bennett's law office and the land titles building, she had been a frequent visitor to the *Eye Opener* office in the months before the wedding. However, this union seems to have had little effect on Edwards and, except for a few random mentions in the *Eye Opener*, she was a closed part of his life.

Because of his well-established reputation as a humorist, Bob Edwards was encouraged about this time to bring together some of his best writings in an anthology. Not satisfied with a purely editorial task, Edwards also added new stories and jokes, often embellishing the tales published a decade earlier. The result of this effort was the ninety-page *Bob Edwards Summer Annual*, a soft cover, pocket-sized book which was published in 1920. Selling for sixty cents a copy, it was snapped up by *Eye Opener* fans all across Canada, and enjoyed a particularly brisk trade among the news vendors on the CPR trains.

Heartened by the success of the venture, Edwards entered into an agreement with the Musson Book Company of Toronto to publish and distribute additional copies of the magazine. As a result, the *Summer Annual* appeared regularly each year for the rest of Edwards's life.

On many occasions, Bob Edwards had also been asked by political parties to join their ranks and to run for office. He had always resisted the temptation, preferring instead to take a neutral stand from which he could strike more effectively against the inequities of the political system. However in 1921 he finally succumbed, running as an independent and easily winning a seat in the Alberta legislature. Some measure of Edwards's popularity can be discerned from the fact that without advertising or public speaking tours, he polled the second largest vote in Calgary in a field of twenty candidates.

He sat for only one session of the legislature, commenting wonderingly, "Isn't it remarkable, here we are in the legislature and McGillicuddy is in hell?" But even before he wrote those words, Edwards's health was failing to such a degree that he had been obliged to go to Vancouver for a complete rest. He made only one speech in the legislature, his maiden address, in which he condemned the devastating effects of the liquor traffic and prohibition. It was a subject which he knew all too well.

By the summer of 1922 he was a very sick man, publishing his last issue of the *Eye Opener* on July 29. Three and a half months later, on November 14 he died at the age of fifty-eight. Mourned across Canada he was the subject of numerous tributes and editorials, all extolling his genius as one of the nation's leading humorists and social reformers.

A short time later his widow established the Bob Edwards Publishing Company and tried to carry on the *Eye Opener*. His eastern publishers also continued to glean stories from his back issues and they published posthumous editions of the *Summer Annual* in 1923 and 1924.

But everyone knew that Bob Edwards and the *Eye Opener* were one and the same. Gradually the effort to keep the newspaper and *Summer Annual* alive became something of a farce. At last the weekly newspaper ceased publication and all rights were sold to an eastern publishing house. There a cheap girlie magazine became the final and tragic beneficiary of a lifetime of Edwards's literary skills. As late as 1933 the Bob Edwards Publishing Co. of Montreal was still grinding out a pulp magazine of dirty jokes and cartoons under the title of *The Eye Opener*. It was a far cry from the proud and defiant journal which had been a part of Canadian life for twenty years.

But the original *Eye Opener* survived the tawdriness of its shallow imitators and Edwards's reputation as a humorist and literary genius emerged unscathed. As editor of his "great moral journal," he had been a social conscience of the Canadian community. Far ahead of his time in matters of political and social reform, his writings have remained as a tribute to a lifetime of devotion to his fellow man. At the same time the pages of the *Eye Opener* reveal Bob Edwards's unique gift—the ability to make people laugh.

DAVID SUZUKI

A passionate defender of the environment, DAVID SUZUKI embraces
every means to let us in on his knowledge. Suzuki is a scientist with the
gift of being able to make science accessible to the populace, through his
prolific writings, as a convincing presenter of television documentaries,
and more recently on the world wide web.

In recent years, if you've been able to look beyond the media obsession with
celebrity, violence and sex, you may have begun to realize that the planet is under-
going cataclysmic and unprecedented change. Ironically, in 1992, the year the
largest gathering of heads of state in human history met at the Earth Summit in Rio
de Janeiro to take concrete steps towards a sustainable future, the Canadian government was forced to acknowledge the unthinkable: the vast shoals of northern cod that
had supported people for hundreds of years had all but disappeared. Since then,
record floods have hit Quebec and Manitoba, flash fires spread across Alberta, and
an ice storm ravaged parts of Ontario and Quebec, knocking out electricity for weeks.
Rates of breast and testicular cancer, asthma and lymphoma have reached epidemic
levels and continue to rise. Hurricane Mitch wiped out thousands of people in
Central America while heat waves killed 700 people in Chicago and thousands in
India. Insurance companies have paid in the 1990s close to four times the weather-
related claims in the entire decade of the 1980s. Can we continue to believe these are
all just random, isolated events?

But the media have been mesmerized by the spectacular rise in Dow Jones aver-
ages, megamergers and record profits, as well as the catastrophic disintegration of

economies from Japan to Brazil. Rachel Carson's seminal 1962 book *Silent Spring* created an enormous wave of awareness and concern about the environment that grew to a peak in Rio in 1992. But since then, the economy has become our dominant preoccupation. We are bludgeoned by the relentless mantra of buzzwords like globalization and free trade, debt and deficit, competitiveness, profitability, inflation and interest rates. So where are we heading? As we approach the end of a millennium, the only way we can gain an intimation of where we are going is by reflecting on where we have come from.

I was born in 1936, when the human population of the entire planet was around two billion. In my lifetime, the number of human beings has tripled. In the year of my birth, the population of Vancouver was 253,000, of Calgary 83,000, and Toronto 645,000. Back then, more than 95 per cent of the world's forests were still intact and pristine while vast areas of Africa, the Amazon and Papua New Guinea were yet to be penetrated by people from the industrialized world. As a child in British Columbia, I hiked through virgin forests, drank from any creek without a second thought and ate raw food pulled directly from the soil or off a tree.

My family moved to London, Ont., in 1949 when the city had a population of 70,000. We had been impoverished by the war and I spent a lot of time fishing in the Thames River to help feed the family. For me, it wasn't work. Walking the banks of the Thames, I had some of my most memorable experiences with nature. My grandparents owned a farm just outside the city where I spent many happy days hunting fresh-water clams or turtles in their creek or watching foxes and pheasants in the fields. Often, I would stop off at a nearby swamp where I would find salamander eggs, catch frogs or collect insects. Those were magical times, imprinting an indelible love of nature that led to a career in biology.

Today, I return to a very different London, a rapidly growing, vibrant city that boasts more than 300,000 inhabitants. But the Thames River is so polluted, people recoil in horror at the notion of eating a fish from it. The only things my grandparents' farm now grows are highrise apartments, while the creek runs invisibly through underground culverts. The magical swamp that captivated me as a boy is covered over with an enormous shopping centre and large parking lot. So where do London's youth find their inspiration today? From grazing through malls filled with consumer items, playing Nintendo games or surfing the Net? The world of young people now is a human-created one that celebrates the inventiveness and productivity of human beings. But there is no way that human ingenuity can match the incredible wonder, magnificence and inspiration of the natural world four billion years in the making. That is not a put-down of our species; it is simply a recognition of the complexity and interconnectedness in nature that we barely comprehend.

Human beings are a remarkable species. We emerged along the Rift Valley in Africa a mere quarter of a million years ago. In evolutionary terms, we are an infant species gifted with a complex brain that is our major survival attribute. That brain conferred curiosity, memory and inventiveness, which more than compensated for our lack of speed, strength or sensory acuity. Today, we have become the most numerous and ubiquitous mammal on the planet.

In this century, our species has undergone explosive change. Not only are we adding a quarter of a million people to our numbers every day, we have vastly amplified our technological muscle power. When I was born, there were no computers, televisions, jet planes, oral contraceptives, transoceanic phone calls, satellites, transistors or xerography, just to mention a few. Children today look at typewriters, vinyl records and black-and-white televisions as ancient curiosities. Taken together, this technology has dramatically increased the impact of each human being on the earth.

In the second part of this century, one of the great insights from biology resulted from the application of molecular techniques to examine specific genes within individuals. To our amazement, when a creature such as a fruit fly was studied, genes were found to exist in many different forms. Even though such species were highly evolved to occupy specific environmental niches, they did not become homogeneous;

instead, they maintained a wide array of gene forms. The phenomenon is known as genetic polymorphism, and we now understand that this is the key to a species' resilience. Over the broad sweep of evolutionary time, the environment is constantly changing. A genetic combination that might be well-suited for one environment might not do as well when conditions change, while other, less favourable gene forms might flourish under the altered conditions. So long as the species as a whole carries diverse genes, combinations better suited to the new circumstances can be selected out when conditions change.

In the same way, it is thought that species diversity within ecosystems, and ecosystem diversity around the world, help to explain life's incredible tenacity under different conditions and volatile surroundings. Planetary conditions have changed tremendously over the four billion years that life has existed—the sun is 25 per cent hotter, poles have reversed and then changed back, continents have moved and smashed together, ice ages have come and gone—yet species have not only survived, they have flourished, and much of that is due to diversity. The converse of genetic polymorphism is monoculture; that is, the spreading of a single genetic stock or species over a broad area. We have learned expensively in fisheries, forestry and agriculture that monoculture creates vulnerability to new infections, disease or altered environmental conditions.

Human beings have added another level of diversity, namely culture, to the equation of adaptability. It is diverse cultures that have enabled our species to survive in so many ecosystems, from the Arctic to the equator. In this wonderful array of cultures, there were many different notions of wealth, purpose in life and cosmic meaning. Today, that has changed dramatically: one kind of economics has become the dominant preoccupation of societies around the world and globalization of that economy is hailed as the source of all wealth and material well-being. This notion is based on perceiving the entire planet as the source of resources while all people in the world form a potential market. But if we live in a finite world, then all resources have limits and prudence demands that we recognize the existence and extent of those limits.

No one person, company or government sets out to deliberately trash our surroundings, yet the collective effect of human numbers, technology and consumption is corroding the life-support systems of the planet. That pronouncement is not the rant of an eco-catastrophist; it is the conclusion reached by leading members of the scientific profession. In November, 1992, more than half of all living Nobel Prize winners signed a document called "World Scientists' Warning to Humanity" that began with this stark statement: "Human beings and the natural world are on a collision course. Human activities inflict harsh and often irreversible damage on the environment and on critical resources. If not checked, many of our current practices put at serious risk the future we wish for human society."

Scientists are extremely cautious when making pronouncements to the general public, so this was a most unusual alarm call. The warning went on to list the areas where the crises exist and the measures needed to avoid a catastrophe. The document then grew more ominous and urgent: "No more than one or a few decades remain before the chance to avert the threats we now confront will be lost and the prospects for humanity immeasurably diminished." It is puzzling to me that we seem frantic to know the most intimate details about O.J. Simpson, Diana, Princess of Wales, or Monica Lewinsky and consume pronouncements by Bill Gates, Larry King or Oprah Winfrey as if they are gospel. But when more than half of all Nobel laureates warn of an impending but avoidable disaster, we are too busy to take notice.

Humanity has repeatedly demonstrated a capacity to respond heroically and immediately to a crisis. Hurricanes, floods, fire or earthquakes elicit remarkable responses. After Pearl Harbor, there was only one choice in North America, to respond and win. There was no debate about whether we could afford an all-out war effort or what the results of not responding might be. In biological terms, the globe is experiencing an eco-holocaust, as more than 50,000 species vanish annually and air, water and soil are poisoned with civilization's effluents. The great challenge of the millennium is recognizing the reality of impending ecological collapse, and the urgent need to get on with taking the steps to avoid it.

But our obsession with economics has become an impediment to taking appropriate action. I have often been told, "Listen, Suzuki, we have to pay for all those parks and environmental cleanups. We can't afford to protect the environment if we don't have a strong, growing economy," or words to that effect. That sentiment flows from a belief that the economy provides us with all of our products, from food to oil to manufactured goods. This is nonsense, of course. Everything that we depend on, whether it is cars, popcorn or computers, comes from the earth and will eventually end up going back to it. It is the biosphere, that thin layer of air, water and soil within which life exists, that creates the earth's productivity and abundance that, in turn, make economies and our lives possible.

But now, ignoring evolution's priceless lesson about the value of diversity, we are monoculturing the planet with a single notion of progress and development that is embodied in the globalized economy. As all nations rush to carve out a place in this construct, we tie our entire future to it. But what if, as many believe, it's based on mistaken notions or assumptions? What will we have to fall back on?

It is widely believed that trade enables human beings to exceed the ability of a certain region to support its inhabitants. Thus, Canadians can acquire Panamanian bananas, Turkish rugs or Japanese electronic products by trading for them with resources or products that are plentiful in Canada. But the reality is that we still require the earth to generate our food, clothing and shelter and to absorb and detoxify our wastes. Trade enables us to co-opt someone else's land to provide goods for us. Adding up the total amount of land (and ocean) required to provide our annual needs, ecologist Bill Rees of the University of British Columbia has calculated that every Canadian (and inhabitant of an industrialized country) now requires the production from seven to eight hectares. If every human being on the planet aspired to a comparable level of prosperity, it would take between five and six more planets! Even if we ignored the entire developing world, we in the wealthy nations already consume more than the earth can provide sustainably. We are blinded from seeing the alternate ecological imperative that demands that we pull back and slow down.

I suggest the following thought exercise can help to get our priorities in order. Imagine that you have lived a full and rich life and are now on your deathbed. As you reflect back on life, what memories fill you with happiness, pride and satisfaction? I suspect it will not be the latest designer clothing, a huge house, a sport utility vehicle or a Sony entertainment centre. In fact, what makes life worthwhile and joyful is not "stuff" that can be bought with money. The most important things are family, friends, community and the sharing, caring and co-operating together that enhances the quality of all of our lives.

There are several reasons we are failing to see the urgency of what is happening. A few of them are:

1) Most people alive today were born after 1950 and thus have lived all their lives during a period of spectacular, unprecedented and unsustainable growth and change. But for most of us, this is all we've ever known and it seems normal. Rapid change also brings rapid collective forgetfulness, and memories of what the world once was quickly fade.

2) Most people now live in the human-created environment of big cities where it's easy to believe the illusion that we have escaped our biological dependence on the natural world.

3) The explosive increase in information shatters the world into fragments devoid of the history or context that might explain their relevance, importance or significance. In order to attract attention, stories or reports become shorter and increasingly shrill, sensational or violent.

4) Political "vision" is focused on re-election and fulfilling the special demands of campaign funders. Political promises are contradicted with little fear of reprisal

amid the cacophony of immediate crises and short-term electoral memory.

5) In a global economy freed from the constraints of national boundaries or regulations, the search for maximal profit in minimal time has little allowance for long-term sustainability of local communities and local ecosystems.

6) The great public faith that "they"—scientists and technologists—will resolve our problems is simply unwarranted. While technology can be impressive, our knowledge of the complexity and interconnectivity in the real world is so limited, our "solutions" have little hope of long-term success. For example, we have no idea how to replace or mitigate thousands of species now extinct, substitute for pollination once done by insects killed by pesticides, or repair the ozone layer.

We can't carry on with business as usual if we wish to avoid an increasingly uncertain and volatile world. The signs are everywhere. But if "experts" lack credibility, try talking to any elder about what fish, birds or woods were like when they were young. Then extrapolate ahead from the changes they have lived through to the kind of world our children and grandchildren will have if we continue along the same path.

What are our real basic needs in order to live rich and fulfilling lives? I believe there is no dichotomy between environmental and social needs. Hungry people will not care if their actions endanger an edible species or an important habitat. Unemployment, injustice or insecurity lead to desperation and the need to survive at all costs. To protect an environment for future generations, we have to build a society on a foundation of clean air, water, soil and energy and rich biodiversity to fulfil our biological needs; we have to ensure full employment, justice and security for all communities to serve our social needs; and we have to retain sacred places, a sense of belonging and connectedness with nature and a knowledge that there are cosmic forces beyond our comprehension or control, to satisfy our spiritual requirements. Then, we can work on the best kind of economy to construct from there. Right now, we seem to be trying to shoehorn everything into the constraints dictated by the economy without establishing the fundamental bottom line.

JAMES GRAY

JAMES GRAY recognised that Prairie dwellers carried many
misconceptions about their own recent history. Drawing on
his journalistic career, and often on his own experience of
salient events, he penned opinionated popular histories of
Prairie issues such as prohibition and prostitution which will
continue to inform generations to come.

The name of the game was whisky. Whisky was the force which impelled the American fur traders into the Canadian west; and it was the liquid lorelei that lured the Indians to the trading posts and their own destruction. Whisky kept the embers of American annexation smouldering in The Dutchman's bar in Winnipeg in the 1860s and it hurried the dispatch of the North West Mounted Police to the western plains to evict the American whisky traders; whisky fuelled the engines of the political machines and corroded their steering mechanisms; whisky oiled the escalators to political success and greased the skids to oblivion.

From Winnipeg to the Rockies, whisky kept the prairies in a ferment for fifty years. Other causes flared brightly for a decade or two and expired. The crusade against whisky went on and on. The Prohibitionist zealots may have let their attention wander occasionally to the espousal of woman suffrage, the eradication of prostitution, or the adoption of the Single Tax. In the end they always came back to the anti-whisky crusade, usually trailing converts picked up along the way from the other movements. It was natural that this would be so. For the deeply religious Methodists, Baptists, and Presbyterians who pioneered the settlement of the west, strong drink was more, much more, than a challenge. Whisky to the fundamentalist Protestants was what pork was to Muslims and Jews, animal flesh was to Hindus, and coffee and tobacco were to Mormons. Not only was booze an abomination to their religion, it was both a millstone grinding on their business interests and, in the rural areas, a threat to their physical existence.

For sheer intensity of conviction and staying power over the long haul no other prairie mass movement ever equalled the Prohibition crusade. And yet the excitement and the political infighting that marked the long assault on the demon rum was hardly more boisterous than the uproar that developed after Prohibition became the law of the land. Then, as governments occasionally did their best to enforce the law, they were heckled continually by the Prohibitionists. While the Temperance spokesmen were demanding more adequate enforcement, clutches of doctors, druggists, lawyers, judges, and free-lance assuagers of the public thirst were conspiring to reduce the law to absurdity. Out of all this there developed a bootlegging industry that kept the newspapers supplied with headlines and provided both Wets and Drys with oratorical ammunition with which to bombard the nearest legislature.

Time, as it has a way of doing, has worked its magic in creating a Prohibition era mythology out of the polemic flotsam drifting in the backwaters of aging memories. Uncountable thousands of western Canadians are convinced that Prohibition either was foisted upon the country by the Borden government during the First World War or was the result of granting voting rights to women while the men were off at war. As a corollary there is the belief that an outraged and enlightened populace voted out Prohibition at the first opportunity. It is believed that Prohibition, in the words of a C.B.C. interviewer, "turned Saskatchewan into the rum-running capital of the world", and as a result broke down law enforcement and ushered in an era of corruption, violence, drunkenness, and debauchery.

There is little foundation in fact for any of the legends and in some of them not even a grain of truth. Not only did the people of the prairies vote for Prohibition with unbounded enthusiasm in 1916, they returned to the polls with equal zest four years later, long after the troops were home, to vote to stem the flow of booze across provincial borders. And when, three years still later, they again returned to the polls to vote for government control as a substitute for total Prohibition, their verdict was defiantly against any return to the *status quo ante* of wide-open bars. The rum-runners, contrary to legend, were usually the personification of restrained circumspection. They seldom arrived for their cargoes before nightfall, and were nowhere to be seen with the coming of dawn. That there were infrequent robberies of country banks along the American border cannot be denied. No evidence can be produced, however, to connect the bank robbers with the rum-runners.

As for the legendary failure of Prohibition, it not only ushered in the most law-abiding era in prairie history, it marked the end of the maleficent impact of wide-open boozing on urban family life. The pauperizing effect of the pre-Prohibition saloons on the working class of the frontier cities is difficult to document specifically, but would be as difficult to exaggerate. All too frequently on paydays and holidays downtown streets became animated replicas of Hogarth prints into which it was unsafe for women and children to venture.

All this, the factual as well as the fictional, was preordained by the nature of the country, the nature of the people, and the pattern of settlement that developed. Which of the three ranked first in importance would be difficult to determine.

* * *

Unlike the other provinces, Alberta's major newspapers did not join the Dry campaign. The *Edmonton Journal* and the *Calgary Herald* enthusiastically attacked the proposed legislation. Both newspapers largely boycotted the mass meetings being staged by the Drys and the *Journal's* editorial page in the latter days of the campaign was given over largely to attacking the Drys. It closed its letters column to communications from either Drys or Wets, while the *Herald*, on the other hand, opened its column wide to the pro-bono publicos attacking the Prohibition law. *Journal* reporters, who did cover some of the small-town meetings, filed reports which had little resemblance to those written by the *Edmonton Bulletin, Calgary News-Telegram*, or *Calgary Albertan* reporters. The *Edmonton Bulletin* gave columns of space to Temperance meetings which the *Journal* ignored, and the *Journal* gave generously of its space to opposition meetings the *Bulletin* ignored.

The most shattering journalistic surprise of the campaign was the embracement of the Prohibitionist cause by Bob Edwards, the notoriously well-lubricated editor of the Calgary *Eye-opener*. To his wide circle of drinking companions, it was an "et tu Brute" betrayal that passed all understanding. Yet Edwards was far from alone among alcoholics who worked on the side of Prohibition. A *News-Telegram* reporter, in a survey of the town of Brooks, noted that the town drunks were all working hard with the Prohibitionists. They too were convinced that if the temptation were far enough removed their troubles with the Devil's brew would vanish.

LISE BISSONNETTE

The irascible publisher of *Le Devoir* and committed Quebec separatist shocked her readers on August 5, 1998 by announcing her departure from the paper to join La Grand Bibliothèque du Québec. This translation of LISE BISSONNETTE'S farewell column in *Le Devoir* examines her sense of the similarity of objectives between newspapers and libraries.

Lise Bissonnette

It is impossible to call firm a decision where doubt is so strong and will stay with me forever. I made it, in the end, for simple and personal reasons. Because what I supposed, in my mind, to have been a seven year term when I accepted the position of publisher of *Le Devoir* in 1990 had already been extended by one year this summer and I felt it was time. Because the proposal to raise from the heart of Montreal the Grande Bibliothèque du Québec came at almost exactly the same date as I was asked to return to the paper and to its head eight years ago, and the project evoked the same urges: an innate desire to serve where ideas are served, in one of the infinite spaces between writing and reading; a hunger, almost physical, for building and creating; the pleasure of living in constant transformation; a taste for a break in the bit of routine I did have here in my office, which fortunately is no longer a crisis management area; the firm conviction, which I have held and nourished for a long time, of the danger of repeating oneself as a professional news analyst, and of the necessity of a change of guard; the will to defy dispersal, both the most seductive and the most frustrating law in the newspaper business; the confidence to know that *Le Devoir* is in good shape, so that I can freely and without fear move on, away from it.

The split is intense but will be less extreme, to tell the truth, than it feels at this moment. There is a link between the assignments I took on at the helm of the paper and those that await me. At least that is my sense.

Essential to the role of publisher of *Le Devoir*, editorial writing requires a global view of Quebec and its environment. In July 1990, at the time I started working again at the paper, the Meech Lake Accord had been defeated barely eight days earlier and the premier had declared Quebec "free of its destiny." The national question, which has been *Le Devoir's* founding question, seemed to be presented on a totally clean slate. Insofar as the fundamental duality of Canada was believed in, any last hopes to bring this vision of duality into form in a mutually respectful or at least amicable relationship had just been dashed, and it became clear we needed to find peaceful ways to assert our autonomy. This basic analysis remains my own. Sovereignty, to my mind, is not something for which Quebec was predestined. Sovereignty seems to me necessary because of the direction that a majority of Canadians want legitimately to impose upon a country whose ideal will never again correspond to the ideal which a majority of Quebecers share despite their diverse political allegiances and which *Le Devoir* has continually defended. The meanderings of the last eight years have since put their marks on this once clean slate, the debates, the committees, the commissions, the Canadian referendum followed by the Quebec referendum, not to mention the day to day changing features of the federation; all that may have influenced my perception of the strategies but never, bottom line, invalidated the findings of 1990. Since then, under the effects of both its revised Constitution and its cultural and social evolution, Canada has nurtured a vision of itself which has some doctrinaire appeal but is not becoming to Quebec's distinctness and will end up undermining it.

It is one thing to refuse that vision, as Quebec did when voting down the

Charlottetown Accord, it's quite another to come up with a better plan. We're looking for it. I have looked for it here. The trap that Quebec is coming up against, in this regard, seems to me to be set from within its own borders. And I am not referring to the extreme indecision of the 1995 referendum on sovereignty-association. I am thinking of our internal blocks, which I have so often discussed in editorials over the last twenty years. Quebec has certainly changed tremendously over these last two decades; it is unrecognisable having caught up in almost all of the quantifiable ways which we hardly dared dream of at the beginning of the Quiet Revolution. Francophone incomes now equal and often surpass those of anglophones and other cultural groups. Ownership and management of Quebec businesses are no longer foreign worlds to us. Public infrastructures, from the James Bay facilities to the universities to the museums, now cover almost the entire province. The universities are overflowing with a student body whose rate of graduation is now favourably comparable to those of our Canadian and American neighbours. The regions define the direction for their own development and are becoming dynamic parts of the country rather than burdens. Every person in this province could compose an extensive, incontestable list of the improvements made by a society which, liberated from its inhibitions or fears, and led quite simply by its ambition, will never again look like a minority.

Any blocks, then? Yes, and all the more cruel because the successes hide them. Overflowing universities, which as a young planner at the University of Quebec I could not have imagined, make us overlook the plight of thousands of young people who leave school in the middle of adolescence and whom we dismiss coldly as losses, not only abandoning them to the streets and unemployment, but also leaving them strangers to the many intangible benefits and the incomparable personal satisfactions which come with knowledge. They account, according to official projections, for at least 15% of the population, these young people who will not complete their secondary studies. The explosive rejection which welcomed last year's report on the general state of education, because it proposed a return to the ideal of equal opportunity, thus calling on us to address first this forgotten group, disturbed me more than any political shock. How have we been able, in educating ourselves as we were encouraged to do, to come to deny more or less consciously this advantage to so many others? It could be the perverse effect of the evolution of an educational system which had to surpass existing levels of superior studies in the scientific, technical, financial, and business fields, which it did with truly enormous success—a success with echoes abroad—but which has treated with unforgivable lightness, from the beginning to the end of the educational process, all those kinds of studies that make us thirsty for other values, for self and for other. And for the community.

Thus Quebec, which naturally produces creators of culture, considers there are too many of these creators because the art lovers and consumers are not numerous enough to make a connection. Thus Quebec seeks everywhere the root causes of its abnormally high rate of unemployment without realising that the answer lies, in part, in the very low intellectual aspirations of its youth. Thus Quebec, when it examines its own political future and its relationship to the world, has so much difficulty understanding the facts of its past and its present situation and the means it could certainly master to bring about its own future. Such is my profound conviction of the extreme and persistent challenge of cultural democratisation, that I must go work alongside the people whom I have so scrutinised, so supported, sometimes criticised but whose purpose I have always deeply valued. Theirs is the world of learning and cultural delight, which the Grande Bibliothèque du Québec will lead me to frequent, at the same time setting myself the task of even better understanding it and of furthering its progress. I entered into my adulthood at the beginning of the Quiet Revolution, I know that anything is possible.

And I admit, here, to having been pushed directly by my work at *Le Devoir*, which has got its finances in order and had its own technological revolution all the while offering lively, diverse, intelligent, often challenging material to its readers, but which still seeks and always will seek a higher number of readers. One of my predecessors assured me that this number would grow automatically and significantly with the level of education; he was wrong and that's an enigma. About the nagging question of *Le Devoir's* modest circulation, I have always refused to console myself that despite the decline, now worldwide, of sales of daily newspapers, our numbers at least have remained the same. The late Fernand Dumont was right when he presented the issue in parliamentary commission as a symbol of our collective cultural challenge. It is right that after having shared in the prestige of this unique paper, I would go, quite simply, to work toward the development of reading in Quebec. We know, you and I, what worlds it opens.

The last lines of this post script recall my first thoughts when weighing my decision. Despite what I have written in the annual reports, despite the evidence I have provided over the years, I have never said just how much your paper exists out of a collective effort. A business like ours knows its clashes and disagreements, notwithstanding what I find to be a general amiability. But I have had proof thousands and thousands of times that everyone on our team intensely shares the elevated objectives of *Le Devoir* and draws a unique pride from them. That is why I have insisted on printing all of their names, every single day, opposite the editorial, in the heart of the publication. I have also recruited or worked alongside or met and always loved to read, over the course of these years, more than a hundred regular or temporary contributors whose generosity has never ceased to amaze me.

As for my closest colleagues, the best testimony that I can give to them is to repeat that I have confidence in tomorrow and after. I have felt, in all senses of the word, their capacity to ensure the longevity and vitality of *Le Devoir*. I thank all those who served on the board of directors of *Le Devoir* over the course of these eight years and who turned it into a cheerful place of shared successes, as well as all the investors who believed in us, all the advertisers who had and will continue to have the wisdom to advertise with us, and all the shareholders assembled under the Foundation of *Le Devoir*, another object of my gratitude. And I could not leave here without reminding everyone, and teaching some, that if I have had energy, often good ideas and sometimes the courage to implement them, I owe it first and foremost to my life partner, whose dedication to *Le Devoir* surpasses even my own.

As for the readers of *Le Devoir*, they will always remain for me the most intelligent, the warmest, and the most animated community of people, a kind of family with whom I share the deepest of bonds. To all those who live at *Le Devoir* or around it, to all those who are associated with the paper and who love it, I entrust to you the tasks of reading it and of encouraging others to read it so that it will continue to grow. It has the capacity and the merit to do so. But in the end we are all guarantors of its life and of its freedom.

ANDY RUSSELL

A lifetime in the wilds of Alberta and British Columbia—first
guiding and trapping, then photographing and writing—
produced an outspoken advocate for the environment.
ANDY RUSSELL'S quietly thoughtful books force his readers
to consider their own intimate relationship with nature.

If there was one important thing that we learned from our parents and grand-parents, it was the value of honesty. Nobody is totally honest, but there are various levels of this virtue, and we were imbued with the need for it. None of our family were very religious according to the creed of any church, perhaps because of our remote and virtually wild surroundings. We did go to services on occasion, but it was not a habit, and when we offered prayers, it was in a very quiet way. Consequently with me religion was a very personal part of my life that I have shared with very few and imposed on nobody. While at first I saw God in the image of man, I later came to know God as the spirit of all things—everything growing and alive, every rock, hill, and mountain.

The Bible was a book that I read at first with interest, and wonder, and later with some question. For it dawned on me at a very early age that it was written by men, and men are prone to make mistakes and twist the truth to meet their own ends. My mother, upon being questioned about biblical discrepancies, assured me that the Good Book, as she called it, was never intended to be taken literally. Its true meanings, she assured me, would be revealed in good time if I continued to study it. I must confess my studies have been limited, but now I can see what she meant.

Looking back, one thing surprises me and has always made me wonder; although she followed the creed of the Baptists, she never had us baptized in any church. It was her belief that nobody should join a church until they were sure which one was best for them. This complicated my thinking for a long time and led me through a tangle of soul-searching. It is something that baptism at birth circumvents, for the youngster who grows up belonging to a church has no such problem, and if he or she accepts the doctrine of that faith without question, it undoubtedly has great comfort in most cases.

But in observing those who unswervingly accept the beliefs of purgatory, the unqualified role of being a sinner, and the prospect of hell and the rewards of heaven, I have found a variety of traps. Among those of my acquaintance who are the most habitual church-goers, there seem to be many who really fear death. Why should anyone be afraid of death if there is real belief? Most of us have a strong sense of self-preservation, but a terror of something totally inevitable is not a frame of mind going with much real faith in anything.

The religious teachers who have impressed me most in my life are the quietly articulate ones with the generosity of spirit to be priests and two or three more were Protestant. One of the latter was a minister of the United Church of Canada, a most accomplished and convincing speaker, besides being a very sunny personality. It was he who moved me, without any real persuasion, to join that church with my entire family, including my wife, four sons, and baby daughter.

Because of the nature of our guiding business, which took us out on mountain trails in summer, we could not attend church then. In winter thirty-five miles of road and bad weather limited our enjoyment of services. But I was active, and for a while it seemed my quest for a real doctrinal faith was at an end. We made our contributions and knew some satisfaction. But then I was appointed to be a steward, a promotion in the hierarchy that eventually involved me in the building of a new church meant for visiting members in Waterton Lakes National Park. There I learned that being a member of a church and becoming part of its business activities are two very different things—something that rapidly became evident to a point of some personal disenchantment.

Maybe I was asking for too much in treating religion as a kind of security blanket to warm me when I required solace in dealings with other people. In any case, I was still troubled, and this led me to join a Bible-study class that met twice a week with the minister. My old friend, the minister who had inspired my joining, was gone to another parish and his successor was a different man altogether. He too was articulate, but at times we found him a bit patronizing and arrogant—attributes that could be forgiven in small occasional doses in the hope that perhaps he would eventually become sufficiently self-assured in his new post that he would not find it necessary.

But one evening during a class, he read to us from the Bible and then proceeded to explain the meaning of the passage. At this point I do not remember the actual point of reference, but I vividly recall that my son Charlie asked why he felt that this was true. Our minister looked at him with evident disapproval and replied very sharply and shortly, "Because I say it is true."

The study period was adjourned shortly after, but the atmosphere was spoiled. When Charlie, who suffers fools with even less tolerance than I, declared that he was through, I could not blame him, and made no attempt to persuade him otherwise.

Upon returning home I asked myself over and over what I hoped to find by being involved in the Church. It nagged me, disturbed my peace of mind, and generally wiped out any vestige of comfort received. One day I was walking alone and the problem was still with me. Going up to a big tree on the slope of a hill overlooking the mountains, I put my arm around it and just stood there drinking in the beauty and the power of the scene spread out under a brilliant blue sky, where clouds were chasing each other like white spume on the wind currents. Suddenly, I was aware of an energy flowing into me from the tree, a power that spread into every part of my body. It completely cleaned me of any doubts and self-recrimination, and my path was as clear as spring water. Any real or imaginary fear of anything was gone. I was personally finished with the hypocrisy of so-called Christian churches and as free as the mountain wind.

I knew then that God is in everything—plants, animals, earth, water, air, and sky. This is the belief of the Jews, and also of the old tribes of the North American Indians—two of the oldest religions on earth. Many Indians have gone back to their original beliefs quite simply because of the contradictions they have encountered in their dealings with us. They believe that all life is involved with the sun, earth, air, and water—a tremendous spiritual power combining to assure all living things of a continuance. They were taught that when they killed an animal they should keep only one-tenth and give the other nine-tenths away to other people. In our Christian missions, we taught them to keep nine-tenths and give the rest to the church.

For a long time our law said that Indians could not purchase or consume any kind of alcoholic drink, but under cover we have always sold it to them for many times what it was worth. When they were finally allowed to buy liquor, beer, and wine—legally—I remember my friend Pat Bad Eagle going into the government store at Pincher Creek and with great aplomb selecting a jug of cheap wine. When the clerk told him it would be three dollars and fifty cents, he stood tall in his moccasins, with his long braids hanging down from under his hat, and with great dignity spiced with unmistakable humor said, "Huh! The price has gone down. I have always paid fifteen dollars for it before!"

I am not an atheist, but it appears to be a mistake for me or anyone else to cleave to written words without question. As a writer, I am too often aware of my own shortcomings to ever assume that what I choose to say is always right. The best of us can only try to communicate our observations and feelings, and hope that our message moves people to think for themselves, even if they disagree.

PATRICK WATSON

PATRICK WATSON is an innovator. As a broadcaster and journalist he pushed beyond the conventional style of news coverage with programs like 'This Hour has Seven Days'. In his continuing quest for more discrimination in programming for Canadians, Watson's *Macleans* Millennium Essay is a pointed look at a national television channel.

Patrick Watson

Here's a great millennium project for Canada. Let's build a public television system. We could use one. It could he an instrument to help restore the ancient and useful idea that there is such a thing as a Public Good, to recognize that Canadians have important things to say to each other and to do with each other. Television might be more usefully employed in that way than just to sell stuff to consumers.

Older readers will recall that for some years the CBC offered an authentically public television service. But then, under the presidency of Pierre Juneau from 1982 to 1989, commercial considerations began to loom larger. Whenever there was a financial shortfall, instead of trimming, say, the vast wasteful overheads at head office in Ottawa, the English and French networks were instructed to sell more advertising. As this was fairly early in the multichannel age, it would have been the right time for CBC-TV to develop a totally distinctive voice. Instead, it began to compete with and look more and more like its commercial competitors, trying to be something for everyone. And for nearly 20 years now, its preoccupation with ratings and advertising revenue has fatally skewed both content and style. It has largely lost its identity and almost totally lost its constituencies. Despite carrying more Canadian-made programming than ever, too many viewers confuse CBC-TV with those competitors.

Over and over again I hear things like: "Say, did you catch that great documentary film last night?"

"What channel?"

"CBC, I think. Or, no, wait a minute. Was it Global? Oh, no! I know! It was History Television, or ... well, I'm not sure. But it was really great."

It's partly the failure of the CBC to create a distinctive service, partly the success of the Canadian Radio-television and Telecommunications Commission, Telefilm Canada and the Canadian Television Fund in putting Canadian-made shows on commercial screens throughout the system. Audiences can see on History Television, Discovery Channel, Bravo!, Global, CTV, etc., publicly mandated programs that look like programs on the CBC.

CBC Radio, on the other hand, is still a public service for Citizens. The capital C here is not casual. In my vocabulary the word Citizen is a term of respect. To say that CBC Radio is a public radio service for Citizens means that it is designed to serve people who care about the country, who want to be involved, to know their fellow citizens, to know about the national life across its multifarious spectra, to have something cogent to say about where we go and how we get there. To that end they want song and story, information and comedy, nonsense and faith, conversation and performance, aspiration and fear, accountability and challenge, that speak to us out of our shared experience as a nation. A genuine public television service would deliver such material at places and times we can count on. Its only purpose would be service, its programming choices determined only by that thing called the Public Interest, and never by the commercial or other partisan interests. CBC Radio, though cruelly starved for resources, still reliably delivers a public interest service that no other broadcaster duplicates. It has a constituency. CBC-TV no longer has one.

Politicians see that all across the Canadian television system there are Canadian-made programs much like what the CBC offers. They also see that, when CBC-TV's budget is cut, almost nobody, except people with vested interests, complains. And so they understand that closing down CBC-TV would not be much of an electoral liability, especially if part of the savings were redirected via the funding agencies, such as Telefilm Canada and the Canadian Television Fund, to increase the amount and quality of Canadian offerings on the commercial broadcasters and cable services.

Some of the specialty cable services are now doing excellent work of a kind that once made CBC-TV unique. Because their programming is distinctive and coherent, they can attract loyal audiences. But the specialty cable services are not *public* broadcasters: they are revenue-driven, depending on popularity and advertising. This leads even the best of them to carry some programming that has no intrinsic value but can be bought cheap to fill out the schedule.

I hasten to add that popularity is important. The early days of CBC-TV were often stuffy, self-indulgent, concerned only about the importance of its subject matter, indifferent to presentation and the special needs of television. Some programmers were insufferably arrogant and superior, a bit like some TV producers and editors today, except that they didn't care much whether people watched. If you watched, that proved you too were superior; if you did not watch, well, it wasn't the programmers' fault. Such a posture was as irresponsible as the one that led to rigged talk shows—it has largely vanished. But so has the ethic based on serving the audience. Serve the audience has been replaced by get an audience. And while you cannot serve an audience if it's not there, you're not likely to provide much service if your only concern is numbers. The objective of much commercial television is to numb viewers into a state of mind that welcomes advertising intrusions instead of rejecting them.

This is a highly developed craft. CBC programmers are often as good at it as other North American broadcasters. But advertising revenue as the prime objective damages the kind of thoughtful and generous programming that the CBC still does from time to time. It's inimical to long-form documentary or drama of integrity because it forces structural breaks that have nothing to do with the requirements of the narrative or dramatic line.

It seems that most viewers accept such interruptions. They use television for escape, for narcotic, for reassurance that war has not started or pestilence broken out, or to prove in the workplace that they are up on the latest celebrity gossip.

But there is another kind of audience, people who feel there's a tacit contract with broadcasters that goes like this: "I, the viewer, will pay attention as long as you, the broadcaster, are enlarging my world and being truthful with your material." Such people are offended by violations of subject matter and of respect for their own judgment, and few are willing to waste the time that television advertising consumes.

Except for people in the public arena, or in the industry, I know very few serious-minded Citizens who use mainstream television much anymore, except for movies, the odd special, occasionally a newscast. The specialty services are different. Cable broadcasters like Bravo! and Discovery Channel appear to be winning loyal viewers. The numbers are small, but it is evident that there are people who want quality, and are willing to pay a subscription fee to get it.

An important Canadian component of that quality television is paid for by publicly mandated funds. But when it is distributed among many channels it doesn't appear to viewers as part of a public effort, something we did as a nation. Something that responds to the need we have to do, together, things in which we have a stake, to build instruments of consensus, of our collective life as a national community, instruments that belong to us, to which we can point with pride, and which respond to our declared national values.

The public discourse of the Canada I grew up in, which for six of those formative years was preoccupied with the 1939-1945 war, was richly strewn with the words "we" and "us" and "together." Together we could endure, survive, triumph. Such words have disappeared from the public discourse; our national leaders seem preoccupied with market values and fiscal probity, matters we used to think belonged in the world of taken-for-granted, but have now been elevated to the ranks of myth and shibboleth. And in those ranks they do not function as stimulants to national pride or unity, or to a sense of common concerns or objectives or pride.

The then-minister of the interior of France, Jean-Pierre Chevènement, said a couple of years ago, addressing the traditional French dislike of immigrants and prejudice in favour of old ethnic stock, that it would be better to define Citizenship as "sharing in a common project." Sharing in a common project! Five simple but electrifying words. And think how important having a common experience of our country must be if we are to recognize our common project when we see it.

That's what a public television service needs to be: a common project. It needs to reflect Canada's diversity of place and people, language and ethnicity, of land and space, of ambition and intent, in a way that allows us to use the words "we" and "us" meaningfully. This is not a matter of earnestness and furrowed brows. It has as much to do with a *This Hour Has 22 Minutes,* a *Royal Canadian Air Farce,* a Celine Dion, a *King of Kensington,* as it does with documentaries and news.

It is also a matter of being inventively responsive to the changing winds of national life. Advertising prevents this even more than it prevents the reflection of diversity. CBC-TV claims, of course, that it is such a reflection. So why does it no longer have a loyal constituency? Simply because the reflection is so partial, so diluted, so narrowed by advertisers' requirements that there is little room for experiment, for real innovation, for risk. And one of the important forms that risk and innovation used to take—a readiness to respond rapidly to perceived need—vanished long ago.

It was common as late as the 1970s when the then-head of TV current affairs, Peter Herrndorf, inherited a tradition in which program heads made decisions and didn't nervously refer upstairs all the time. It was a time when, if the country was in a spasm, a programmer could say: "Look, we need to open up the network for a couple of hours this week to deal with this." In the October Crisis of 1970, CBC-TV stayed on the air all night. You didn't need to be on cable to be part of a nation on alert.

* * *

Now. What should this new public television system look like? Here are some principles and considerations that a government should declare when it asks a think-tank to design a new system and a model program schedule.

The service must be distinctive. In an age of specialty channels, it makes no sense for a broadcaster to try to be everything. So the new public television agency must be the Canada Channel: programs of quality—from nonsense to profundity, from fantasy to science, from goofiness to tragedy. Instead of cashing in on tried-and-true formulas, the public television broadcaster will take chances and break new ground. The primary criteria should include service, relevance and an ongoing invitation to know and take part in the life of the country. They should invite creative solutions to the challenges of content, distribution, finance, experimentation and risk-taking, and respect for both audiences and participants.

There must be room for the refined arts: the specially arts channel Bravo! with its very small resources has done impressive, innovative work in raising Canadians' awareness of the performing arts, and there's more to be done. Yes, those arts generally reach only a relatively small group of people, but they are people who make a lot of decisions; they pay a lot of taxes, they teach in our schools and do community service, they head governments and corporations, they contribute a lot to the national life. And they get little back on their television screens.

And the high arts ripple out and refresh the popular arts: classical dance nourishes popular dance; experimental serious music finds its way into the pop stream and enriches it. No Bach, no *Whiter Shade of Pale*. No classical string quartets, no

Eleanor Rigby. No Richard Strauss, no *Phantom of the Opera.*

Producers must be enjoined to make all programs as attractive as possible to a wide audience, consistent with the integrity and authenticity of the material. A public service using public resources has a political, moral and social obligation to be comprehensible and accessible to the widest possible audience.

Recognizing the large number of alternative attractions in the television spectrum, program schedulers must give audiences several opportunities to see new programs within the immediate period of their first release. This would entail a sophisticated and well-researched pattern of repeats that does not penalize the viewer who wants to see other programs on other channels within the Canadian system.

Next, is the issue of distribution. Based on a recommendation from a cable system designer, Sruki Switzer, the CBC engineering department was asked some years ago to consider putting the entire TV transmission service on satellites. Five or six transponders could serve the whole country and protect regional interests and time-zone needs by feeding local cable services. For the small percentage of homes out of reach of cable, it was argued, it would be cheaper to subsidize their purchase of direct satellite dishes than to maintain hundreds of terrestrial transmitters.

The reader will not be astounded to learn that CBC engineering, asked to evaluate a proposal that would have radically reduced its size and budget, did nothing. The underlying question is, does a public television system need plant at all, studios, transmitters and so on? Or could it do what it has to do using existing facilities as carriers? That is, could the existing commercial broadcasters and cable services be instructed to open up regular time slots for programs from a public television agency that owns no hardware at all?

It is at least conceivable that the best Canadian instrument for the new century would be a public television agency that commissions all or most of its programs from independent producers, deploying public funds to make programs that existing services would be obliged to carry. When the existing CBC-TV disappears,

Newsworld will lose its main source and will die as well. Our new public television agency could fund and set standards for a news service, probably as a separate, independent organization, supplying both the main service and, if viable, an all-news channel. The agency could, in effect, own or control a number of periods on commercial broadcast and cable services, regularly scheduled time slots that viewers could count on to be carrying the distinctive public service. Part of the compensation to those broadcasters would be a straight fee for service as a carrier and part the increased advertising revenue available to the rest of their schedule with a major competitor (the CBC) no longer in the advertising game. In any case, large publicly owned establishments of real estate and buildings and transmitters are no longer appropriate. Those facilities exist in a profitable private sector, which ought to be deployed, partly for pay and partly for public purpose, in the execution of a public television strategy.

I favour a combined approach: a distinctive "All Canada Channel" extended by a pattern of second windows amongst the other channels, something that has begun to happen already.

I think a national convention should be held to bring together the practitioners who are out there on the cutting edge of television, cultural development, entrepreneurship and social policy. Moses Znaimer of Toronto-based City TV has done more for innovative television than anyone else in Canada, so he should be empanelled. Evan Soloman, host of *Future World* on Newsworld, is far ahead of most of his colleagues in his thinking. Trina McQueen has made Discovery Channel sing, and long ago, as head of information programming at CBC, was brilliant at defining the role of a public broadcaster. The national convention should also canvass the recently adolescent coveys of genius who are designing Web sites and thinking the unthinkable.

This assembly or think-tank would not be a parliament, not a representative caucus: that's a recipe for paralysis. This must be a group of communications inventors. Put them together in a room. Give them a clear mandate in broad strategic terms. Their job is not to declare the purpose of the new public TV service—that's up to Parliament—but to devise the method and the machine. So give them a set of objectives about what the country needs and tell them they have six weeks to come up with a structure, a distribution system, a statement of guiding principles and a budgeted model program schedule.

It can be done. In 1984, a tiny task force, operating under the same kind of directives, designed a workable, low-cost second CBC channel to be known as CBC Weekend, only to have the CBC board lose its nerve and shelve the project.

It will need a name, this new agency. One is tempted to call it something like the *Canadian Broadcasting Corporation*—a name that once conveyed a grand dream and perhaps could do so once again.

IV. ON PASSIONATE DEVOTION TO AN IDEA

KNOWLTON NASH

For decades an authoritative face on the evening news—foreign
correspondent, anchorman, executive—KNOWLTON NASH
continues to push for intelligence in all journalistic media. A strong
believer in the possibilities for television and other modern media,
Nash, like Bob Edwards, is wary of the too-easy slide into triviality,
form over substance, and sensationalism.

W alter Lippman once wrote that "journalism is the last refuge of the
vaguely talented", a comment that proved he had never met Bob
Edwards.

Some journalists, indeed, may have delusions of adequacy, but Bob Edwards had
a unique combination of journalistic talent, philosophical purpose and just plain
mischief. His *Calgary Eye Opener* was never dull, let alone "vague". Edwards' fingers
danced across the typewriter keyboard clawing away at the "establishment", and
sometimes his fingers would seem like talons producing sharp-edged commentaries,
accusations and exposés that infuriated the high and mighty. He once wrote that the
Premier of Alberta was one of "the three biggest liars in Alberta". The other two,
he said, were Robert Edwards "gentleman" and Bob Edwards, "editor". Unlike
today's *Frank Magazine* which is always scandalous and occasionally accurate, the *Eye
Opener* reflected the approach of Lincoln Steffens and H.L. Mencken rather than
Walter Winchell and Matt Drudge, and then Edwards added a generous helping of
his particular brand of caustic invective and satire. He was a "muckraker" in the

best sense of that word, and he knew there was a lot of muck to rake. To get people's attention focussed on serious issues, he knew he had to make his copy lively, and that he certainly did.

I often wonder what Edwards would think of the button down journalism that occupies so much of the news business today. Likely he would have been chagrined at the gentrification of most journalists who have moved from the beer parlour and pretzels of yesterday to the cocktail lounge and tofu of today. Likely, too, he'd try to find some middle ground between establishment media and *Frank*, something provocative and irreverent, cutting through "spin doctored" news and devoted to educating the public to reality. Unquestionably, he would have disdained much of the contemporary mainstream news focus on trivia and on those seeking their fifteen minutes of fame. Almost certainly, he would have rumbled in indignation at the concentration on presentation instead of substance that permeates so many newspapers today. He would have positively thrown up looking at the flimsiness of much of our broadcast news. Surely, though, he would have hailed the Internet with its iconoclastic irreverence and "in your face" journalistic potential. I can just see him, sitting in some paper-strewn office cubbyhole, puffing on his cigar, a drink at his side and banging away on his computer, muttering to himself, "Take that!" and sending off his latest diatribe to the Bob Edwards Web Site in Cyberland.

While he believed journalism should be taken seriously, if skeptically, he surely would scoff at the reality today that news has become the most powerful product in the world. Take what we do seriously, he undoubtedly would say, but add that the news business must also be fun ... the most fun you can have with your clothes on.

As an old-fashioned, hard-drinking newsman, he probably would revel in the comment by Baltimore Editor H.L. Mencken who once said, "journalists represent the human character in complete disintegration." In fact, as an often debt-ridden alcoholic, he'd likely take it as a compliment. Edwards once announced his endorsation of prohibition by saying, "What I propose to prohibit is the reckless use of water." He knew only too well that the two absolute essentials to survive a Western Canadian winter are whisky and anti-freeze and he made sure he had a good supply of at least the former. Even so, he supported prohibition in a 1916 referendum.

The illustrious recipients of the Bob Edwards Award have included everyone from René Lévesque to Allan Fotheringham and having been personally acquainted with those two in particular, I know Edwards would have empathized with them. Although, almost as impossible as it may sound, he likely could have out-drunk and out-shocked all of the recipients put together. Like most recipients of the Bob Edwards Award, he knew that the road to good intentions is paved with Hell, and he enjoyed the roadblocks along the way. Edwards certainly enthusiastically endorsed the philosophy of my poetic namesake, Ogden Nash, who once wrote in a couplet: "Home is Heaven and Orgies are vile, but I do like an Orgy once in a while." His interpretation of "once in a while" may have been a bit more liberal than most.

It's said that old broadcasters, like me, never die, they just lose their frequency, but while, in time, Edwards may also have lost his frequency, he never lost his journalistic potency.

Politicians were a particular target for Edwards' caustic commentaries and he concentrated a lot of his sarcasm on the verbal dexterity and multitudinous promises of politicians. He shared the feeling of Canadian humourist Stephen Leacock who once noted that it's simply in the nature of a politician to promise a bridge in one election and then promise a river to run under it in the next.

Edwards once defined a statesman as a dead politician, and then he added that the country needs more statesmen. And unconventional as always, he ran for office in a provincial election in Alberta in 1921 and won. He, of course, ran as an independent.

In Bob Edwards' day, and today as well, there was and is a love-hate relationship between politicians and journalists. We spend a lot of time with each other. Then, as now, although we may lie in the same informational bed, there always is barbed wire between the sheets. Certainly journalists today, as in Bob Edwards' day, see a lot of political silver tongues in leaden minds. What would Edwards, for instance, have made out of former Newfoundland Premier Brian Peckford's comment who is alleged to have offered a cure for unemployment in Newfoundland by announcing he would create hundreds of jobs for thousands of Newfoundlanders. Or what would Bob Edwards have made of one-time Nova Scotia Premier Roger Bacon who also spoke on unemployment, by saying, "If these people weren't unemployed, they'd be working today."

One-time Toronto Mayor Allen Lamport would have warmed the cockles of Edwards' heart with his put down of hecklers: "I deny the allegations and I defy the alligators!" I remember once duly taking note of a debate at the United Nations Security Council where the Arab and Israeli delegates hammered away at each other all day long until finally, in the late afternoon, a tired and frustrated American Ambassador rose from his seat and demanded, as he said, that "the Arabs and Jews settle their differences in a good Christian manner!"

One of the most biting criticisms that I've ever heard of journalists came from former President Jimmy Carter's Press Secretary Jody Powell who said political journalists are "like those who watch the battle from afar, and when it's all over, come down from the hills to shoot the wounded." Actually, it's hard to think of a politician today who doesn't think that way from Ralph Klein to Jean Chretien.

There are more than enough wounded politicians these days, and it's true that in politics, nobody stops to pick up the wounded. But like Bob Edwards nearly a century ago, most of us in journalism today are not trying to "shoot the wounded". What we're trying to do, as did Bob Edwards, is to sift through the rhetoric of our political leaders to try to find reality. Too often, though, our leaders are not so much interested in reality as they are in perception. That re-emphasizes the importance of journalism to reflect reality as best we can, as clearly and effectively as we can, just as Bob Edwards was doing in the *Calgary Eye Opener*.

I was chatting about this at lunch not long ago with an old colleague and former CBC foreign correspondent, Morley Safer, who for years has been a Correspondent for the CBS program 60 Minutes. Before 60 Minutes, he had been an outstanding CBS reporter in Viet Nam, more effectively and accurately reflecting the reality of that war than anyone else. So much so that President Lyndon Johnson tried to get him fired because, Johnson said, "He's a communist." When repeatedly assured by his aides that Safer was a *Canadian*, not a *communist*, Johnson replied that, "well, anyway, God damn it, he knew something was wrong with the son of a bitch!"

The trouble was, of course, that President Johnson simply did not want to hear the reality of Viet Nam because it profoundly differed from the perception he wanted the public to have about what was going on over there. He didn't want to hear facts that would wound his theories.

But facts and strong opinions were Bob Edwards stock in trade and he was never hesitant to unearth and express them. One lesson Edwards teaches today is that politicians have to recognize that disputing reality is never going to change reality. We stake everything on a rational dialogue of an informed public and the challenge for those of us in the business of news is to strive relentlessly to come as close as we possibly can to providing a fair reflection of reality so people can understand and cope with that reality.

A journalist's loyalty lies first of all with the public in general and that was the audience Bob Edwards was addressing. Journalists, in effect, are agents for the public in reporting what's going on in front of and behind the scenes. We provide context and we may occasionally note where some leaders are economizing on truth, as happens all too often these days.

And that, of course, was what Bob Edwards was seeking to do, as well. He did it by lampooning, by humour, by sometimes outrageous caricatures, but always with a serious purpose.

A lot of years ago, Lord Byron wrote, "A small drop of ink ... makes thousands, perhaps millions, think", and Bob Edwards' drops of ink in the *Eye Opener* were designed to do just that. With his audacious style, he prodded people to think. He knew that the secret to effective journalism is to make the important sound interesting and not make the merely interesting sound important.

Deservedly, Robert Chambers Edwards, born in Edinburgh, raised in Alberta, has become a journalistic legend in Canada.

JACK WEBSTER

In 1978, at the peak of a 40 year career in radio journalism, JACK WEBSTER considered retirement. Instead, tempting terms induced him to move to the bright lights of his own TV talk show where Pierre Trudeau was his first interview. Webster's relentless style daunted many a lesser interviewee but Webster always insisted on the journalistic tradition of getting at the truth.

W hat kept my interest from flagging was politics. I turned to Prime Minister Pierre Trudeau for help in kicking off my initial television broadcast. Although besieged at the polls and on the verge of defeat, he made time for me. He always did.

The best I ever did with Trudeau, who is only a year younger than I, was break even. Maybe once I had him on the run. He was such a cold, Jesuitical debater that I eternally had to remind him that I was asking the questions. I wasn't going to answer his questions. But he was the only man I was ever truly nervous about interviewing in all my years in radio and television.

Early on, I regarded Trudeau as the most arrogant, supercilious SOB I had ever met as a politician. But he became my one true political guru even though our first meeting was nasty, brutish and short.

Trudeau only entered national politics in the mid-1960s and was chosen Liberal Party leader, thence Prime Minister, because the backroom boys had to find a television personality. They didn't know what or whom they were promoting.

He was frankly lukewarm about the monarchy, Commonwealth and other Canadian-Anglo-Saxon articles of faith when he gained power. He sauntered around the official residence barefoot, attended official receptions in sandals and cravat, and delicately sniffed roses while seated in House of Commons debates.

Trudeaumania swept Canada. Men and women literally fought to touch the hem of his garments. He undoubtedly had a charisma which enveloped even this hard-nosed reporter who told him on television coast to coast, "You'll either be the best or worst prime minister Canada has ever had."

Trudeau was not pleased with my attitude because he had little time for nosey reporters and basically distrusted the press—with reason when one remembers his part in fighting press monopoly in Quebec in the early 1950s.

I disliked Trudeau after our first meeting when he was only a cabinet minister. He was so god-damn arrogant.

We were at a press conference in the social suite of the Hotel Vancouver. Jack Wasserman and I were there together and we took offence at all the Liberal hangers-on who joined the press conference. Wass and I put our feet down: "Get all these flacks out or there ain't going to be any press conference," we said.

We won our point.

During the ensuing questions a young student said to Trudeau, who was then minister of justice and running for the Liberal leadership: "If you become leader of the party will you withdraw from NATO?"

He gave an answer.

The young U.B.C. kid said, "In other words, you'd pull out."

"That's not what I said," Trudeau replied.

I said, "Let me try Mr. Trudeau. IF YOU BECOME PRIME MINISTER WILL YOU PULL CANADIAN TROOPS OUT OF NATO?"

He gave me an answer. I said, "See, the U.B.C. kid was right. You gave me the same answer you gave him and I interpret it the same way."

So our first meeting was a little bit abrasive.

* * *

Trudeau could not have been aware then what a hard line I had come to take on drugs. If a drug trafficker was jailed for seven years in prison, I'd be on air saying the court was soft—he should have got seventy! I did a program on the toll it was taking in Vancouver by interviewing forty families who had lost sons and daughters to heroin addiction.

I believed smoking marijuana should be a firing offence in the schools. I talked to one 17-year-old kid potted out of his head. He had no money, no hope and no future. He told me he came from Kamloops and had become hooked because of the glamorization of the drug culture by the Beatles, the Rolling Stones and other rock groups.

Trudeau eventually clarified for me his stand on the issue in a subsequent interview. "Decriminalization, yes—in the sense that we don't want a person condemned for mere possession to have a criminal record that will follow him or her for the rest of his or her life," he said. "Decriminalization in that sense, yes. Not in the sense that it will no longer be an offence of any kind to possess and use marijuana. There will be some restraint, but it won't go into your criminal record or result in a jail sentence."

I pressed him: "But you would expect a big increase in the use of marijuana among young people who say, 'Oh, it's decriminalized; it's legal. It's not a danger.' That doesn't worry you too much, marijuana?"

"It would worry me if I was smoking it or I saw my kids smoking it," Trudeau said. "I think the effects on the mind are not determined any more than the effects of alcohol and a lot of other drugs. I think if you can stay away from it, it's better."

"And if you can stay away from all of them, so much the better," I added.

"So much the better," he agreed.

I always took a hard line on drugs. In the beginning, as far as I was concerned, junkies should be quarantined until they died or kicked the habit. Later, I came to see addiction as a more complex problem that was deeply rooted in prevailing social conditions.

Trudeau never did change the law.

In the early days, all Trudeau and I ever seemed to do when we met was argue. I would accuse him of trying to censor press conferences; he'd accuse me of attempting to hog all of the questions. Touché!

After one dust-up, I overheard him say to an aide as he left: "Why does that man hate me?"

"Webster doesn't hate you," the aide replied.

"But he's always yelling at me," Trudeau said.

"Webster's always yelling at everybody."

After some years in government, Trudeau lost his early socialist fervour and became a fairly orthodox Liberal in many ways. He would probably describe himself as a pragmatist. He appeared from nowhere at a time when it looked as if the nation might well be split apart by French Canadian separatist influences, and he may well be the man of the century for keeping this nation in one piece for as long as he did.

Quibbling about Trudeau's mannerisms and peccadilloes goes out the window when you realize he was the only Canadian federalist at the time who could talk equally to six million French Canadians and fourteen million non-French. He was so bilingual he wrote poetry in both languages. He rode Anglo-French feelings with the touch of a master. He coped, too, with political potentates who controlled ten provinces, from wealthy British Columbia to the underprivileged Maritimes and touchy, sensitive Quebec, where one wrong move brought outrage from the rising tide of separatists.

Trudeau was the first Canadian Prime Minister since Glasgow's John A. Macdonald a hundred years before who was brutally frank on major issues facing

Canada. I'm sure Trudeau made the White House shudder at his frankness.

To his shame, Trudeau did move Canada away from the traditional British Parliamentary system. He increased his personal staff vastly and in many ways is to blame for the problems that plague us today. But Canadian governments for the previous twenty years had been filled with an awful lethargy. It was wonderful to have a swinger with such a vast selection of glamorous girlfriends as Prime Minister instead of stodgy diplomats and mouthy politicians.

Remember Eva Ritting-Hausen—a jetsetting blonde he lunched with in London? She left telling everyone it was "love at first sight." The next night he was out with a brunette. "I don't feel snubbed at all," insisted scorned Eva. "I think he should enjoy himself."

We were willing to take a chance on Pierre, married or single. I grew grudgingly to respect and finally to admire the man.

We had several memorable exchanges over the years on radio. One in particular was the way he dealt with an ambush I planned. I arranged for a man who was manipulating the unemployment insurance plan to call and embarrass the government. "I just called to thank you for your generosity over the past year," the fellow began.

"Does that have a sting in it or is that sincere?" a wary Trudeau asked.

"It's got a bit of a sting in it actually, I've been collecting $85 a week UI for the past ten and a half months."

"You'll be cut off soon and have to go back to work," Trudeau said.

"No, I'm in a special category, I can carry on until January 26th to be exact. But my wife has been earning $500 a month and we've been living extremely well in the West End and I hope something positive can happen for me in a job sense. I've been looking for work, honestly looking for work, and I've been through the Canada Manpower grind. I even took the psychological tests to see if I'm a sane, all-Canadian boy. Which I am. They recommended I go into sculpting or pottery. I have a wife and a child to earn a living for. I'm 27, I graduated from high school in 1964 and I have two years of university."

"Don't give me all the details," I interjected, "but what are you going to do with the money you saved on UIC?"

"We just got back from San Francisco and we're planning to go to Hawaii at Christmas time," the caller said proudly.

"Have you refused any jobs Manpower offered you?" Trudeau asked obviously irritated.

"Yes," the man replied, "I refused two. I refused to load bricks on a lorry at $1.95 an hour and I turned down a job for $400 a month as a delivery boy."

"There's a lot of guys getting a free ride on unemployment insurance and we're cutting them off at a very high rate," Trudeau warned sharply. "So if that's your case I'd be very interested in having your name. Please send it in. I guarantee you a job within ten days and if you don't take it, I guarantee you'll be knocked off. And if you go to Hawaii, it'll be as a bum."

I gave Trudeau the man's name after the show and I learned a few days later that he had been offered and accepted a job at the Post Office.

* * *

There was one Trudeau-Webster exchange, however, that the eastern media and Trudeau-bashers will always hold against me. It was when I asked him when he would retire on February 20, 1981. He gave me that famous Cheshire-cat grin and said "Jack, I'll make you a deal. You and I retire together, O.K.? When you get out of this game, I'll get out."

I just laughed. A lot of people told me I should have accepted the offer, including the editorial board of the *Globe*: "We trust the eminent west coast broadcaster Jack Webster does his bounden duty and retires forthwith."

They were sure the country would be better for it. I'm not so sure.

JACK PEACH

In weekly newspaper columns and radio spots, JACK PEACH'S infallible memory and warm writing style made Calgary's history dance. Colourful descriptions of local personalities, lively retellings of society happenings, and vivid accounts of everyday life allow Calgarians an enviable access to the city's social, geographic and architectural history.

Jack Peach

Even before Calgary officially became a town, it had a newspaper. *The Calgary Herald, Mining and Ranche Advocate and General Advertiser* made its debut on 31 August 1883. Publishers Andrew M. Armour and Thomas B. Braden were farm boys from Ontario and had been friends since boyhood. Armour had a bit of newspaper printing experience before setting up shop on the frontier with his pal, a former schoolteacher in Peterborough.

They had the backing of Toronto milliner Frances Ann Chandler and an extra pair of hands courtesy of the local mounted police detachment, who loaned them Constable Thomas Clarke, a printer in civilian life. Their printing equipment had arrived on the first freight train to reach Calgary, addressed: "T.B. Braden, end of track." Before 1884 was over, they had moved their little business out of a tent into a shack and had hired Hugh St. Quentin Cayley as editor.

In 1885 Cayley, who had worked for the *New York Herald Tribune*, bought *The Herald*. Armour moved to Medicine Hat to start a newspaper, and Braden, who couldn't get on with Cayley, went to California where he and his wife became an evangelical team. Hugh Cayley stayed here and became notorious for his outspoken opinions.

One such "opinion" was that George B. Elliott, the publisher of a short-lived local rival paper, *The Nor'Wester*, was a childish egotist, a vampire, and a Lilliputian from nowhere! Cayley also took a round out of unpopular local Magistrate Jeremiah Travis, repeatedly calling him an arrogant eastern popinjay. That caper landed him in jail for a couple of weeks, but upon his release he was lionized by the small population, who staged a parade from the barracks to the newspaper office with celebratory stops at the saloons along the way.

In his absence another mounted policeman, G.E. Grogan, ran the paper, which, by then, Cayley had turned into a daily despite the limited number of readers. When a building and immigration boom in the early 1890s came to an abrupt end *The Herald* nearly vanished. In 1894 it was rescued by a bright young English newcomer, John J. Young, who brought it back to vigorous life.

For news, people bought *The Herald*, but for social comment and acerbic wit they bought Bob Edwards's *Calgary Eye-Opener*, which was published at irregular intervals! Edwards had brought his newspaper skills to Calgary via Wetaskiwin and High River.

The Herald's appearance was also a bit patchy. When Thomas Braden returned to work at the newspaper, Norman Luxton (who later founded the Banff Museum) was barely managing to keep it afloat. There was little money to pay bills such as those submitted by the telegraph service that supplied the news. In such cases Luxton would visit the railway station, read the papers carried through town by passengers, then nip back to get the latest into print.

In 1902 *The Herald* was doing well enough to afford the city's first two Linotype machines, which replaced the painstakingly slow job of setting type, a letter at a time, by hand. Back in its infancy in 1883, *The Herald* had complained in an editorial that mail took a month to travel to Calgary from Toronto. In those days the quickest route was by railroad in the United States to Fort Benton, then north by ox train to Calgary. Otherwise mail was sent to the end of the line as the CPR laid its trackage across the continent, and from there, with innumerable delays, had to wend its westward journey through the courtesy of whichever reliable soul was headed this way.

But once the railway reached Calgary it brought with it a fairly reliable telegraph circuit—an improvement in communication that encouraged further newspaper activity. The new kid on the block was *The Calgary News Telegram* (*The Nor'Wester* had disappeared by this time). Though *The News Telegram* had a short life-span, it made quite a splash. On Saturday 14 June 1913 it issued an eight-page "Prosperity Edition," the front page of which featured a lavishly imaginative bird's eye view of a mythical Calgary. That cover was even printed in black, golden brown, and scarlet!

An ornately coiffured woman is swathed in a cloak, her gown bearing a maple leaf brooch. She stands by a cornucopia on a Romanesque marble balcony gazing towards the distant Rockies beyond a skyline of spires, smoking chimneys, freight trains diplomatically labelled CPR, CNR, and GTP. Near a patch of unharvested fields and chunky office buildings stands a grain elevator and silo. A four-storey building bears the modest sign, "Nearly Everybody Reads the News Telegram." More than that, the woman holds at arm's length a copy of *The Calgary News Telegram* bearing a superimposed slogan, "A Great Newspaper in a Great City in a Great Country." This Freudian art work is attributed to the Calgary Engraving Company.

One of Calgary's remarkable newsmen, Fred Kennedy, worked for *The News Telegram*. Fred, an immigrant from Ireland, delivered papers at age twelve and was determined to become a news reporter. This determination had him delivering papers for *The Morning Albertan*, then gobbling breakfast at home in time to get to *The News Telegram* at 8 a.m. for an hour of clipping and filing duties. At 9 a.m. it was off to school, and when that was over, supper, then away again to *The News Telegram* where he did his homework, since it was quieter there than at home. Talk about dedication!

As the Great War raged on in Europe, wounded Alberta soldiers began arriving home. Young Fred, in an attempt to hone his reporting skills, spent much of his precious spare time at the railway station, scene of much news. He was given part-time jobs in the newspaper library and collecting photographs of Calgary war casualties from their next-of-kin. At the same time Kennedy was attending two night classes a week at Mount Royal College preparatory to taking entrance exams for the University of Alberta.

In 1916 Saskatoon newsman George M. Thompson bought *The News Telegram* and moved it into its own new building on Eighth Avenue West between First and Second streets West, opposite the Capitol Theatre. The presses were in the basement, visible to pedestrians through a row of large sidewalk-level windows. The editorial offices were at the top of a short flight of stairs on the raised main floor.

According to Fred Kennedy, publisher Thompson, "was red-headed and wore peg-top pants with a suit coat that reached almost to his knees. He also wore 'American type' boots with exaggerated toe swell, and smoked ill-smelling cigars. He had a large and pretentious private office complete with fireplace. His pride and joy was a huge brass cuspidor that he could hit dead centre with unerring accuracy."

Thompson renamed his afternoon daily newspaper *The Calgary Canadian*, and, in creating it, he inherited Fred Kennedy and managing editor Charles A. Hayden, who later became city editor of *The Calgary Daily Herald. The Calgary Canadian* lived only two years. As a parting gift, George Thompson solemnly presented Fred Kennedy with the giant cuspidor. Fred hadn't the heart to say he did not smoke or chew.

Charlie Hayden found a new berth as senior editor at *The Morning Albertan*. At the end of the war he had Fred join him there. For twenty-four years, Calgary's morning daily was owned and published by William McCartney Davidson, but *The Albertan's* financial status didn't change. When Fred Kennedy was hired in 1919 he was told, "Your salary will be $14 a week, when you get it."

There were several other newspaper ventures over the years, not the least of which was *The Western Standard Illustrated Weekly*. I suspect the war scuttled that brave attempt, for the remnants of a copy I have bear the date Saturday 14 March 1914. It was a sixteen-page newsprint paper in two sections covering the topics of Financial and Insurance, Society, Sport, Business and Building, Motors and Motoring, Theatrical, and Late News. That was just the first section. In the second part were Within the Week and Other Stories, Editorial, Farming Page, Country Life, Women's Section, Stories, Prairie Provinces, and For Our Merchants.

Editor D. Matheson Sr. obviously felt that Calgary was well served with newspapers, for he busied himself tearing a strip off the Calgary Board of Trade for announcing that its secretary was going to publish a newspaper. He suggested that, "If the Board of Trade has so much money it does not know what to do with ... it should hire a good, capable publicity agent to properly advertise Calgary and try and get some new industries." So there!

Clearly Calgary, even way back then, was a city with many loud opinionated voices.

RENÉ LÉVESQUE

Known in Canada as the father of the Parti Québecois and a Quebec separatist, RENÉ LÉVESQUE'S talents were much broader than many of us imagined. As a respected print, radio and television journalist, Lévesque covered world events from Dachau in WWII to the first interview of Khrushchev by a Western journalist.

René Lévesque

Korea—and my gallant hilltop swearers—presided over my coming of age as a journalist. Returning home I discovered that commentators as hard to please as Gérard Pelletier were referring to me as "the revelation of the year." In high places they were also beginning to catch on to the fact that sport isn't the only human activity capable of holding public attention. Without ever equalling the magic of the stadium, the presentation of other sides of life still has the advantage of costing only a small fraction of the television budgets gobbled up by soap operas and variety shows. In addition, the years 1939-45 were the crucible in which the metamorphosis of the new Quebec society was forged. Thousands of young men had left the country and had, like me, changed without quite realizing it. Thousands of women had been shunted by war from offices to factories and were no longer the same as they had been. This unprecedented turmoil was responsible for the rapid disappearance of the old traditional and isolationist Quebec. One of the effects was the awakening of a new curiosity about the distinctiveness and originality of our own people. In song, in theatre, in our first films, we began to discover in detail who we were and to find ourselves interesting.

Whatever the causes, that was the context for the creation of a "feature news service" that I was placed in charge of. It was a mini-department destined to remain microscopic, but a lot of heart was shown by the little team that worked on putting out a daily radio-magazine called *Carrefour*.

* * *

At that particular moment our trade was just being sent back to school to learn the ABCs of television, the appearance of which threatened to put us all on the shelf. For the actors especially it was a disaster. They had been used to playing their parts script in hand for so long that many had completely forgotten how to memorize a role as required in live theatre. After the initial blow had provoked a period of self-examination, little by little there was revitalization and a new public appeared for quality radio. (The other kind, alas, simply continued to fight over the lowest common denominator.) I think I am not alone today in preferring sounds that create their own decor and leave a place for silence to the omnipresent image, the image at any price, of which it is false to claim that it is invariably worth ten thousand words, or even ten seconds of peace.

But let's get back to the fifties and that first generation to slump down for life in front of, or behind, the flickering screen. It was a mass infatuation, such as we've never seen, creating a drug-like dependency that few escape even today because it hits its victims at any age. Our eldest child was three when the thing first erupted into his life. Coming into its presence with that senatorial walk of his, he saw an airplane buzzing across the screen. As soon as it disappeared on the left, he went over to that side of the set, then walked right around it, coming back to us with: "Where'd the plane go?"

What will be the long-term impact of all those images that generations of kids have been served up endlessly for the last thirty years? You'd have to be pretty smart to evaluate that with any degree of certitude, or pretty presumptuous to claim accurate results. One thing is certain, though: almost nothing has escaped this alchemy that hasn't always turned base metal into gold. Education, household routines, the extravagant overpersonalization of politics and sports, all those fields have been affected. How does the dazzling technical evolution represented by these strange windows on the world stack up against the herd-minded superficiality spewed out of them day after day? The danger is particularly grave in a little society like ours where the monster makes short work of subjecting everyone to the same wavelength, with a menu that becomes more imperious than the dictates of any Academy: the next episode of the daily soap (Grignon's *Un homme et son péché*), *Hockey Night in Canada* ("Over to you, Jean-Maurice ..."), and so on.

Here's a memory from those prehistoric times. I had been filling in a little on TV news when one day, in the middle of a blizzard so thick you couldn't see the end of your nose, a Good Samaritan gave me a lift. I soon began to notice him looking at me in a most curious fashion. Finally he couldn't contain himself any longer: "It seems to me I know you from somewhere, but I can't think where."

Not knowing either, I sat in silence until he was struck by a sudden revelation: "I've got it! It's simple. I'm sure I've met you at my house!"

Similarly, Victor Barbeau, an elegant old gentleman whose temper grew shorter as his years grew longer, once reproached me for my lack of good manners in appearing in his living room with a cigarette hanging out of the corner of my mouth.... In those days TV was decidedly a family affair.

As for the mutations that our perspectives and even our senses were to undergo, as early as 1948 I had a striking preview of that. It was in Chicago where I was covering the Democratic convention for the radio; south of the border television was already in power. It's hardly necessary to say that we Canadians were the poor relations relegated to the far end of the table, left to beg for crumbs from the feast that had been laid on for the grand seigneurs of the camera. On the rented set that allowed us at least to be not completely out of it, the day was winding down with the roll call of the delegates. They had reached Missouri and, in alphabetical order, the letter t:

"The delegate from Independence, Missouri … ."

At these words an image bobbed up on the screen of an airport in the Middle West where you could make out a little man hurrying toward his plane.

"President Harry S. Truman!" the announcer intoned triumphantly. If I'm not mistaken, it was the first time two sides of a single news event were spliced together live on the screen. It's old hat now, but that day we found it mind-boggling and my report home was full of the wonder the future held in store.

This was also the beginning of what I might call my American period. It was the politics that interested me first—from Truman to Eisenhower to Kennedy—but also, as often as a chance or pretext occurred, I would cover any other aspect of that enormous cultural stew bubbling away just over the border. Our strikes teleguided from Pittsburgh or Washington, the blood ties that prevented Franco-Americans from completely forgetting us, the German presence whose beer was the Milwaukee flagship, the discreet infiltration and multiplication of Orientals on the West Coast: in short, everything fascinated me in the perpetual movement to the south of us whose rhythm invaded our lives and dissolved the frontier in floods of Coke and tires and V-8s.

Given the fact that my own frontier had been fixed long ago at the Ottawa River, it was easy for me to follow the natural slope of the continent that runs north and south instead of the unnatural east-west line along which Canada is built.

My wartime contacts had only reinforced this preference. Coming back to Quebec in 1945, then again in 1952, each time the temptation had been strong to follow in the footsteps of certain American comrades going home to New York or Boston to carve themselves out enviable situations in the U.S. media world, where the growth potential was geometric. But I realized then that I would never be an export commodity. I was condemned to remain Québécois. This feeling only grew stronger when, on several occasions, I was offered more or less golden opportunities of exile, among them at least one that would have seen me in the federal arena—on the wrong side of the river.

But as much as Canada outside Quebec seemed to me, generally, to be a sad collective grey, the United States never ceased to fascinate me, and this double impression has remained to this day. I had discovered and was belatedly reading up on the Roosevelt years. I don't believe one can ever find, in any place or time, a person who can serve as a model for one's own life, but close affinities often develop with people we admire. Without for a single instant thinking of political action, I began an intensive diet of FDR. In the first place I had been struck by his great communications skills. Listening to those "fireside chats," his lilting voice that scanned the sentences as if they were prose poems, I envied him his gift for capturing attention and creating suspense while using everyday words with chiselled precision. And he used humour so well to disarm or confound his adversaries, for example, during a wicked campaign when he was led to exclaim with just the sigh that was needed, "Good heavens! Next they'll be after poor Fala!" (his little dog, an inseparable companion). Above all I admired the incomparable instinct that permitted this aristocrat to maintain for so long a coalition made up of minorities, blue-collar workers, and the poor. In 1932, thanking the members of his brain trust for the monumental work they had done drafting the complete program of the New Deal, he asked them to resign themselves to seeing their chef-d'oeuvre condensed and reduced to its simplest expression, as concise as a manifesto.

This was what doubtless came to my mind when in 1967 I was writing the text that was to launch the Mouvement Souveraineté-Association and in 1968 *An Option for Quebec*, the second part of which, entitled "A Country that is Feasible," opened with the quotation, "We have nothing to fear but fear itself." These words, which Roosevelt had used to try to exorcise the panic caused by the Great Depression, seemed to me to apply every bit as well to our own colonial apprehensions and complexes.

* * *

I was in a fair way to becoming transformed into a "Yankébécois." South of the border attracted me so strongly I invariably spent the holidays down there, always by the sea, to be sure. At first we went by train to Hampton or Old Orchard Beach to rent one of those vacation shacks whose only merit was that it was two minutes from the beach. Then around 1955, when my salary has reached the stratospheric heights of five thousand dollars a year, I was able to buy a car and expand our horizons. That finally led us to Cape Cod, that eighth wonder of the world whose southern beaches are washed by the warm currents of the Gulf Stream and whose entire shoreline has been wisely turned into a national heritage park, which spares it the disfigurements of so many other incomparable sites from Capri to Acapulco and Miami to Percé. It was there that our three children—Suzanne having joined the two boys and established her reign over the family—acquired a taste for saltwater and seafood while learning English the painless way. And there I return faithfully every year for two or three weeks of thalassotherapy that my Gaspésian organism can't do without, but also to bathe in that society that is so close yet so profoundly different from our own.

Nothing is closer, indeed, than that American democracy one might almost call innate, which springs, like ours, from simple, unpolished people untrammeled by class division who knew how to make the most of the limitless space of a new and almost empty continent. This is the source of that fundamental egalitarianism that gives everyone the conviction or, if you prefer, the illusion that he is as good as his neighbour or, why not, the president. It is also the root of that habit, which puritan virtues have preserved better with them than with us, of working hard without asking for the moon (or even without expecting services as essential as health insurance and a reasonably priced educational system). In everyday life all this makes average Americans the most sympathetic "foreigners" you can imagine, and people you can identify with better than any other.

But this closeness that goes far beyond geographical bonds tends to camouflage the fact that History has given us traits of character that are markedly different. Children of a France obsessed with Europe and rich enough to live unto herself, we were only a handful of settlers at the time of the Conquest. On the contrary, England was poor and seafaring and had shipped a multitude of immigrants to its own colony. On the Plains of Abraham the weight of numbers won the day and eventually won control of the whole of North America. This was accomplished in the United States in the course of interminable campaigns against the Indians marked by a violence that gave rise to the racism and the revolver culture that remain a blight on the country to this day. Independence wrested with the bayonet, followed by a civil war more deadly than any previous conflict, served only to anchor this propensity to rule by force even more solidly.

Pass over a century and wars with Mexico and Spain, 1917-18, 1941-45, and Vietnam, and look at the situation in 1986. American society continues to secrete such violence that its crime rate is the highest in the world. The very strength of the country engendered what Eisenhower called the military-industrial complex whose chief interest is to maintain tension with the Soviets, thus justifying the insane budgets swallowed up in so-called defence—"so-called," because as far as we can see into the future, the U.S.S.R. will never have the temerity, much less the means, to pass to the attack. Russia is poor, and in our day wealth leads the world, not the flag as in times past. At this rate Tokyo and soon the whole of the Far East will be taking over from New York and Chicago. After the transplant that in the recent past removed the heart of the world from Europe to America, another transplant will see it removed again.

Running the risk of turning Central America into a new Vietnam or of locking himself into the unreality of Star Wars, President Ronald Reagan is only disastrously masking this evolution and delaying the need to come to terms with it, a task that will be anything but easy. The inevitable transition will doubtless call forth the greatest of any demonstration the Americans have ever been asked to give of their proverbial powers of adaptation. Scarcely less challenging will be the partial abandonment of the melting-pot philosophy, which may be forced on them yet by bi- or tri-culturalism, as witnessed particularly on the Pacific Coast. The internal evolution of the United States and the relative diminishing of its international importance will reserve shocks and surprises for us that a small neighbour will have to follow very attentively. And it will continue to be a fascinating spectacle.

ALLAN FOTHERINGHAM

ALLAN FOTHERINGHAM'S acerbic wit and clever turn of phrase have chagrined many a subject of his newspaper and magazine columns. Some solace may be taken as Fotheringham, in the manner of Bob Edwards, often includes himself as a target of his humour. Yet always we must respect the right to express one's opinion, however uncomfortable for some.

First, the disclaimer. The scribbler was born in Hearne. Hearne is in Saskatchewan. In Saskatchewan they have winter. Snow. Ice. All that. But this is Toronto. Scribbler wakens with headache. Scribbler never has headaches. Lady of House smells something funny. Scribbler agrees, something funny in air. Lady of House phones brother. Brother knows about things. Sez sounds like gas leak. Find the vent outside house. Open all doors and windows, he sez, as safety measure.

Lady of House, as always, does the heavy lifting. Goes outside with shovel. Starts shovelling in search of vent. Location of vent unknown. Scribbler, a sensitive poet, goes upstairs to computer. On deadline as usual. Possibly behind deadline. As usual.

Neighbourhood children, demon shovellers, join hunt for mystery vent. Four feet of snow. Brother thinks may be carbon monoxide leak from gas furnace. Sensitive poet keeps hammering away at laptop computer. Carbon monoxide one thing. Editors are another.

Neighbour comes by. Wonders why Lady of House trying to dig to China. Lady of House explains sensitive poet upstairs. Can't be disturbed. On deadline. Neighbour is architect. Knows something about houses. Comes in. Sniffs. Orders Lady of House to call 911 immediately. Sensitive poet upstairs remains aloof from fray.

Three minutes go by. Sirens sound. Huge fire truck, size of Prince Edward Island, pulls up. Inhalator truck. Fire captain's truck. A fourth truck. Fifteen firemen emerge. Sensitive poet types on.

Fire captain tells Lady of House worst mistake was to open doors and windows. Must contain gas. Thinks dead raccoon in chimney vent to blame. Raccoon, like Toronto's mayor, probably seeking warm place to sleep. Or hide. Sensitive poet doesn't understand. Doesn't want to. Carbon monoxide? Carbon dioxide? Sensitive poet never did pass Grade 9 chemistry.

Very impressed with firemen. Polite. Disciplined. Try to tell fire captain a joke. Rookie firemen silent. Squad leader silent. Fire captain laughs. Squad leader laughs. Rookies laughs. Sensitive poet thinks paying taxes OK after all.

Next squad arrives. With Geiger counter to check gas. Geiger counter needle goes nuts. Fire captain orders everybody out of house immediately. Sensitive poet races upstairs. Fire captain yells. But got to get laptop. More scared of editors than gas.

House evacuated. Retreat to fire captain's truck. Sit there typing. Show must go on. Feel like ingenue backstage at Broadway on opening night, leading lady being sick. If only cruel editors knew what was going on.

Gas company arrives. Shuts down furnace. Chimney people on way. In search of alleged raccoon. Or Mel Lastman. Whichever comes first. House freezing. Must search for hotel. Firemen wipe up floor before they leave. Lady of House loves them, every single one. Sensitive poet jealous, considers changing professions. Concludes wouldn't work.

Neither sensitive poet nor Lady of House smoke. Fire captain sez if either had lit up, or started fireplace, four houses would have gone to moon. Wonder if neighbours appreciate us.

By now 3 p.m. Sensitive poet and Lady of House, starving, repair to neighbourhood pub for sandwich. Immediately become heroes to the locals since they greatly amused at traffic chaos caused by four fire trucks. Which is why they can't get home. So flee to pub. The alleged raccoon in chimney becomes instant icon. Some think he looks like Mel Lastman.

House now secure, but freezing. Power shut off. Lady of House and sensitive poet return to pick up shaving kit on way to hotel. Lady of House hears waterfall. In basement. Rush down. It's flooded. God damn raccoon strikes again.

Flood rising rapidly to adjoining room where sensitive poet, wisely, has stored his entire literary output since 1908 in scrapbooks in mouldy cardboard boxes. Did Hemingway do this? Poet and Lady of House risk hernias in mad marathon to lift everything to kitchen. Feel exactly like farmers in Red River flood rescuing their pigs from rising waters.

Basement alien territory to sensitive poet. Never been there before, as one recalls. Like never having been to Siberia. Lady of House, she of the heavy lifting, knows that. Talk to chimney/gas people. They, too, astounded. House is 100 years old. Furnace, they claim, must be 200 years old. Looks like designed by Rube Goldberg. And possibly retrieved from Titanic.

Gas furnace must be replaced. Chimney wrecked. Must be repaired at great cost. It now a $4,000 raccoon. The lads in the pub would love it.

Sensitive poet and Lady of House finally find hotel in a city where army and P.E.I. snowblowers have been recruited, after most interesting day of 1999. Stagger in. Fall into bed.

At 5 a.m. hotel fire alarm goes off. Triggered by the usual weekend drunk. Sirens sound. Fire trucks roar up. Lady of House phones the insurance company.

PERMISSIONS

Atwood, Margaret. "Survival, Then and Now", (c)1999 by Margaret Atwood. Reprinted by permission of the author and *Macleans*.

Berton, Pierre. "The Man Behind the Eye-Opener" from *Pierre Berton's Canada,* (c)1999 by Pierre Berton. Reprinted by permission of the author and Stoddart Publishing Co.

Bissonnette, Lise. "Post Script", (c)1998 by Lise Bissonnette. Translated from French by Clare Frock. Reprinted by permission of the author.

Callwood, June. "Mendelson Joe", (c)1999 by June Callwood. Reprinted by permission of the author. An earlier version of this article appeared in the *Globe and Mail.*

Dempsey, Hugh. Excerpt from "Introduction", *The Best of Bob Edwards,* (c)1975 by Hugh Dempsey. Reprinted by permission of the author.

Fotheringham, Allan. "How a Sensitive Poet Met a $4000 Raccoon", (c)1999 by Allan Fotheringham. Reprinted by permission of the author and *Macleans*.

Gray, James. Excerpts from "Belly Up to the Bar, Boys!" and "The Slogan that Won the West", *Booze,* (c)1972, 1995 by James Gray. Reprinted by permission of the estate of James Gray and Fifth House Ltd., Calgary.

Gzowski, Peter. Excerpts from "Robertson Davies, Part II", *The Morningside Years,* (c)1997 by Peter Gzowski. Reprinted by permission of the author and McClelland & Stewart.

Lévesque, René. Excerpt from "Two Superpowers: The Camera and the U.S.A.", *Memoirs* by René Lévesque, (c)1986 by Editions Québec/Amérique. Translated from French by Philip Stratford. Reprinted by permission of the estate of René Lévesque and McClelland & Stewart.

MacEwan, Grant. "Editor and Horse Thief: Peter J. McGonigle" from *Fifty Might Men,* (c)1958 by Grant MacEwan. Reprinted by permission of the author and Douglas & McIntyre.

MacGregor, James. Excerpt from chapter 10, *North-West of Sixteen,* (c)1968 by James MacGregor. Reprinted by permission of the estate of James MacGregor.

Mitchell, W.O. Excerpt from "The Poetry of Life", *An Evening with W.O. Mitchell*, (c)1997 by W.O. Mitchell. Reprinted by permission of the estate of W.O. Mitchell and McClelland & Stewart.

Nash, Knowlton. "Bob Edwards at Large", (c)1993 by Knowlton Nash. Reprinted by permission of the author.

Newman, Peter C. "Saluting the Playwright who became President", (c)1998 by Peter C. Newman. Reprinted by permission of the author and *Macleans*.

Peach, Jack. "Read All About It", from *Thanks for the Memories: More Stories from Calgary's Past,* by Jack Peach, (c)1994 by Audrey Peach. Reprinted by permission of the estate of Jack Peach and Fifth House Ltd., Calgary.

Richler, Mordecai. "Memories of Moore", (c)1999 by Mordecai Richler. Reprinted by permission of the author and *Saturday Night*.

Russell, Andy. Excerpt from "Looking Back", *Memoirs of a Mountain Man*, (c)1984 by Andy Russell. Reprinted by permission of the author and Formac Publishing Company.

Saul, John Ralston. Excerpt from "The Faithful Witness", *Voltaire's Bastards: The Dictatorship of Reason in the West,* (c)1992 by John Ralston Saul. Reprinted by permission of the author and Penguin Books Canada Ltd.

Shields, Carol. "Others" by Carol Shields, (c)1999 by Carol Shields. Reprinted by permission of the author.

Suzuki, David. "Saving the Earth", (c)1999 by David Suzuki. Reprinted by permission of the author and *Macleans*.

Watson, Patrick. Excerpt from "A Project for Canada", (c)1999 by Patrick Watson. Reprinted by permission of the author and *Macleans*.

Webster, Jack. Excerpt from chapter 13, *Webster!*, (c)1990 by Jack Webster. Reprinted by permission of the estate of Jack Webster and Douglas & McIntyre.